Gentle Parenting
with a Twist of
Montessori

Nurturing our Babies to
Preschool Children with
Creativity and Connection

Sara B Hope

To my chickadees and buntings,
my greatest teachers

Table of Contents

Introduction

There's no doubt that parenting is one of life's most rewarding experiences, but let's be honest—it's also one of the most overwhelming. The moment you bring your child into the world, the weight of expectations hits you hard. It's not just the idealized images on social media or the constant stream of advice—it's the pressure from every direction. Family members may offer well-meaning but outdated advice or remind you how *they* did things, making you feel like you're not living up to their standards.

And then there's your own idealism—trying to be that perfect parent you imagined you'd be. The one who never loses patience, always makes organic baby food and creates a perfectly- balanced, stimulating environment. Between family expectations, social media comparisons, and your high standards, it's easy to feel like you're already falling behind, wondering if you're doing enough or if you're even cut out for this at all.

It's a lot to take in, I know. As a mom of three grown children and a grandmother, I've been where you are. When I first became a parent, I felt the same pressures you may feel now—trying to balance my ideals with family expectations and the constant stream of advice from every direction. For nearly a decade, I took a break from my career to homeschool my children, filling our days with principles that embraced the beauty and magic of early childhood. I didn't always get it right, but I learned there's no single "perfect" way to raise a child—only what works best for you, your family, and your unique child.

That's why I've written this book. to share the insights I wish I'd had when I was in the thick of it, to help you approach parenthood feeling more grounded, confident, and capable. By the time you finish reading, you'll have a toolkit full of practical strategies to make life smoother, deepen your connection with your child, and help create a home filled with peace and growth. More importantly, you'll come away confident in your parenting style and decisions, assured that you're doing what's best for your child, your family, and yourself. This journey is uniquely yours, and by trusting your instincts and staying rooted in your values, you'll discover a path that truly works for you.

Being a grounded parent isn't about comparing yourself to someone else's highlight reel. It's about making real-time decisions, grounded in science, instinct, and experience, that will help you become the parent you want to be. Not a perfect parent—because that person doesn't exist—but a present, confident, and connected one. You've already got what it takes; sometimes you just need a little help cutting through the noise and trusting your instincts.

Throughout this book, we're going to look at nurturing from two viewpoints. **Gentle Parenting** and **Montessori Principles.** These two approaches work beautifully together. Each offers a framework and practical ways to build a relationship with your child based on respect, empathy, and trust. Both paths offer strategies for navigating discipline, sleep, play, and all the other daily challenges of raising a young child.

Again, this isn't a book about perfection. Parenting is an adventure. messy, unpredictable, and often downright exhausting. You'll still have moments of frustration, and that's okay. What matters is that you remain committed to your chosen path, even when it feels as though you've hit a brick wall. Because it's also about finding common ground with those around you. Whether it's your partner, parents, or caregivers, developing a shared vision for raising your child can be one of the toughest challenges. Differing opinions and approaches are bound to surface. Creating an approach that works for everyone involved requires patience, clear communication, and an unwavering sense of what's most important to you and your family.

Parenting is a journey, and like all the best journeys, it's full of surprises. Some days will feel like you're winning, and others like you're barely holding it together. Both are perfectly normal. Both are part of the process. Through it all, always remember. you have everything you need within you to grow alongside your child and become the parent you aspire to be.

Enjoy the read and enjoy the journey!

Chapter One

The Science Behind Gentle Parenting and Montessori

These days, gentle parenting is one of the most widely discussed approaches, especially among new parents eager to nurture their children from the beginning in a thoughtful, respectful way. You may have come across the emphasis on empathy and respect that gentle parenting promotes or heard about Montessori's child-centered, exploration-driven methods - but are they just trends, or do they hold lasting value rooted in research?

Both approaches emphasize respect for your child's natural development, guiding them with a blend of empathy, structured freedom, and purposeful interaction. And for many parents, they represent a refreshing alternative to more conventional approaches, building a foundation of trust and mutual understanding from day one.

In this chapter, we'll explore how the principles of gentle parenting and the Montessori methods are supported by academic studies. I aim to help you understand not only why each approach has become so popular but also how each can bring more joy and connection to your relationship with your child as you nurture them from infancy through each stage of their young life.

An Overview of Gentle Parenting

Key Principles and Influential Research

Gentle parenting has gained significant popularity over recent years, particularly with the growing awareness around child development and emotional intelligence. Contrasting sharply with traditional, authoritarian models that prioritize obedience and control, or more recent permissive, hands-off philosophies, it's an approach that emphasizes empathy, respect, and understanding in the parent-child relationship.

With its focus on fostering cooperation and emotional intelligence, gentle parenting seeks to nurture a child's natural development without relying on punishment or rewards as behavioral motivators.

Respect for the Child as an Individual

> "When we help children learn to regulate their emotions, we empower them to build resilience and foster healthy relationships." — Daniel J. Siegel

One of the foundational principles of gentle parenting is *respect for the child as an individual*. Children are seen not as extensions of their parents but as autonomous individuals with unique thoughts, emotions, and needs. This perspective shifts the dynamic away from enforcing authority and towards collaboration and mutual respect. Research has shown that children raised with respect and understanding tend to develop stronger social and emotional skills, which are crucial for long-term mental well-being (Siegel & Bryson, 2016).

The Importance of Empathy

> "Gentle parenting is about creating a loving environment that nurtures your child's emotional intelligence, fostering cooperation and connection rather than fear and obedience." — Dr. Laura Markham

A key tenet of gentle parenting is *empathy*. Parents are encouraged to view situations from their child's perspective, acknowledging their emotions and helping them navigate difficult feelings. Empathy strengthens the parent-child bond and models how children should respond to others' emotions. Dr. Laura Markham's influential study (2012) found that empathetic parenting fosters emotional regulation in children, reducing the likelihood of behavioral issues and enhancing their ability to handle stress.

Compassionate Boundaries

> "Gentle parenting is not about being permissive; it's about being aware of our children's emotional needs and responding to them with compassion and understanding." — Dr. Shefali Tsabary

In addition, *boundaries with compassion* are central to gentle parenting. This approach doesn't advocate permissiveness it encourages setting limits in a way that honors the child's emotions and needs. Boundaries are clear but are explained rather than enforced through punishment. Research by Professor Ross Thompson (2014) emphasizes that when children understand the reasons behind rules, they are more likely to cooperate and develop internal motivation, as opposed to simply acting out of fear of punishment.

Emotional Coaching

> "Respectful parenting means trusting our children to take the lead in their development while providing guidance and support." — Janet Lansbury

Finally, *emotional coaching* plays a crucial role in gentle parenting. Instead of simply correcting a child's behavior, parents are encouraged to help their children label and understand their emotions, teaching them how to process feelings constructively. Studies by Gottman et al. (1997) on emotional intelligence have demonstrated that children guided in this way tend to develop stronger interpersonal skills, experience fewer emotional outbursts, and display greater resilience in the face of challenges.

A growing body of research supports the long-term benefits of gentle parenting. Studies have shown that children raised with this approach are more likely to develop healthy attachments, exhibit better emotional regulation, and have higher self-esteem as they grow into adulthood. For example, a longitudinal study by Coyne, Stockdale, and Nelson (2018) revealed that children raised in empathetic, boundary-respecting households demonstrated greater self-confidence and social competence in adolescence.

> "Connection is the key to parenting; it's the foundation for everything else. When children feel connected to their parents, they're much more likely to cooperate." — Dr. Tina Payne Bryson

To summarize what studies have revealed, by embracing gentle parenting you're committing to a transformative approach that prioritizes your child's emotional well-being and development. By fostering respect, empathy, and compassionate boundaries, you're setting the stage for your child to thrive socially, emotionally, and cognitively. Gentle parenting empowers you to cultivate a nurturing environment where your child can explore, learn, and grow, ultimately building a strong foundation for a fulfilling life.

Whatever the challenges, your choice to prioritize emotional development over mere compliance is a gift that will resonate throughout their lives, shaping not only who they become but also the quality of their relationship with you.

The Montessori Approach

History and Underlying Philosophy

> 'The greatest gift we can give our children are the roots of responsibility and the wings of independence' — Maria Montessori.

Developed by Dr. Maria Montessori in the early 20th century, the Montessori approach to education is rooted in the belief that children are naturally curious and capable of directing their learning.

Born in Italy in 1870, Montessori was one of the first female physicians in the country. Her observations of children led her to develop this unique educational philosophy that emphasizes hands-on learning, independence, and respect for a child's natural psychological, physical, and social development.

Montessori's methods gained recognition and quickly spread beyond her native Italy, influencing educational practices worldwide. Today, Montessori schools are found across the globe, providing an alternative to traditional educational methods.

Respect and Independence

> 'She stands firmly on her own two feet and I just behind her, should she ever need me' — J. Iron Word.

At the core of the Montessori philosophy is the idea of *respect for the child*. This respect is manifested in the belief that children learn best when they are free to choose their activities within a structured environment. Montessori explained that "The first aim of the prepared environment is, as far as it is possible, to render the growing child independent of the adult" (Montessori, 1967). This independence is crucial, as it develops self-motivation and confidence, enabling children to take ownership of their learning journey.

Self-Directed Learning

Montessori also emphasizes *self-directed learning*. In a Montessori classroom, children are encouraged to explore materials at their own pace, engaging in activities that interest them. Research supports this approach, suggesting that children with the freedom to choose their learning paths develop better problem-solving skills and critical thinking abilities (Lillard, 2017).

A study by T.de Vries in 2015 also demonstrated that Montessori students performed better on standardized tests and exhibited higher levels of creativity compared to their peers in traditional educational settings.

Hands-On Learning

Another key element of the Montessori approach is *hands-on learning*. Montessori classrooms are equipped with specially designed materials that are both engaging and educational. These materials promote exploration and discovery, allowing children to learn through experience. Dr. Montessori noted, "Imagination does not become great until human beings, equipped with a little play and a little observation, are able to act" (Montessori, 1949). This philosophy highlights the importance of active engagement in the learning process.

Collaboration and Community

The Montessori approach encourages *collaboration and community*. Children of different ages learn together in mixed-age classrooms, fostering social skills and peer learning. This structure mimics real-world dynamics, preparing children to navigate various social situations. Research by McNerney (2015) indicates that collaborative learning environments enhance social development and foster a sense of belonging among children.

Overall, the Montessori approach is a holistic educational philosophy that values independence, self-directed learning, hands-on experience, and community. Its historical roots and guiding principles offer parents a framework that not only respects the child as an individual but also nurtures their innate curiosity and desire to learn.

Why Gentle Parenting and Montessori Work Well Together

Gentle parenting and the Montessori approach share a foundational belief in respecting the child as an individual and nurturing their inherent potential. Both philosophies emphasize creating a supportive environment that fosters emotional growth, independence, and problem-solving skills.

When integrated, these two approaches can create a balanced framework that not only guides children in their learning but also strengthens the parent-child relationship as they grow.

Respectful Communication

One of the most obvious ways these approaches complement each other is their emphasis on *respectful communication*. In gentle parenting, the focus is on empathetic listening and validating children's feelings. Similarly, Montessori education encourages children to express themselves and engage in dialogue about their experiences.

For example, when a child faces a challenge, a gentle parenting approach would involve acknowledging their feelings and guiding them through problem-solving, and a Montessori perspective would encourage them to explore the issue independently, using available resources in their environment. This dual approach helps children to develop resilience, as they learn to articulate their emotions and develop effective coping strategies when things get tough for them.

Autonomy and Independence

Another area of synergy lies in the way *independence is valued.* Gentle parenting promotes autonomy by allowing children to make choices within a safe framework. Montessori education takes this further by providing a prepared environment where children can freely explore and engage with materials designed to promote self-directed learning.

As a parent, you can create a home environment that mirrors Montessori principles by offering age-appropriate choices—such as allowing toddlers to select their clothes or involving preschoolers in meal preparation. This practice not only builds confidence but also reinforces the idea that their choices matter.

Learning Through Exploration

Both approaches encourage *natural learning through exploration.* Gentle parenting recognizes that children learn best when they engage with the world around them. Montessori classrooms are structured to promote hands-on experiences, where children learn through play and discovery.

You can integrate this principle into daily routines by facilitating exploration during outdoor play, engaging in creative activities, or encouraging curious questions. For instance, if your child expresses interest in bugs, provide magnifying glasses, books, or apps about insects, to transform everyday moments into learning opportunities.

Focus on Emotional Development

> *"A child seldom needs a good talking to as much as a good listening to."* — *Robert Brault.*

The focus on *emotional development* is central to both philosophies. Gentle parenting emphasizes emotional intelligence and the importance of recognizing and regulating feelings. Montessori aligns with this by creating an environment where children are encouraged to understand their emotions and those of others.

You can cultivate emotional awareness at home by modeling emotional expression, discussing feelings openly, and validating your child's experiences. Activities such as reading books about emotions or practicing mindfulness can reinforce these concepts, helping children to navigate their feelings effectively.

As you integrate these two approaches, remember that the balance between gentle parenting and Montessori is entirely a matter of choice. Your approach can evolve based on your child's developmental stages, interests, and needs. For instance, a more structured routine may work better for a young child who thrives on predictability, while an older child might benefit from greater freedom and independence. Trusting your instincts and adapting your style to suit your family dynamics will help create a nurturing environment tailored to your unique situation.

Blend the Two Styles in a Way That Works for You

To summarize, by adding that twist of Montessori to your gentle parenting you can create a rich, supportive framework that respects your child's individuality while fostering their emotional and cognitive growth. This integration invites you to create a home environment where exploration is encouraged, emotions are acknowledged, and independence is nurtured.

Before we move on, I want to reassure you that how you blend these approaches is entirely up to you - and you'll learn as you go along. There's no one-size-fits-all solution - it's about finding a balance that resonates with your family's values and dynamics. As your child grows and their needs evolve, your approach can shift, allowing you to be flexible and responsive.

Again, I want to encourage you to embrace your unique parenting journey, with its many joys and challenges. Trust that by blending gentle parenting and Montessori principles, you're equipping your child with the tools they need to thrive in an ever-changing world.

Reflective Questions

Now that you've explored the ideas in Chapter 1, take a moment to reflect on how these concepts connect with your personal experiences and parenting journey. The following questions are designed to help you examine your own assumptions, deepen your understanding, and identify practical ways to apply what you've learned. Consider your answers thoughtfully, and allow yourself space for honest self-reflection and new insights.

1. Think about your own upbringing—how did your parents' approach to discipline shape your current views on parenting?

2. Which aspects of gentle parenting feel most aligned with your natural instincts, and which feel challenging or counterintuitive?

3. What assumptions or biases might influence how you perceive your child's needs or capabilities?

4. Recall a recent situation where your child's behavior frustrated you—how might leading with empathy have changed your response?

5. What emotions or unmet needs do you notice most often in your child, and how do you currently address them?

6. How comfortable are you with recognizing and naming your own emotions?

7. Reflect on a recent time when your child wanted to do something independently—how did you respond, and what might you do differently next time?

8. What benefits of hands-on learning resonate most with your parenting goals?

Chapter Two

The First Year (0-12 Months)

'As babies we're born blank sheets of paper. Not a mark. As we grow older, lines form, then colors and patterns. Before long the paper is all sorts of brilliant. Like a kaleidoscope, no two exactly alike' — Shannon Wiersbitsky

Understanding Development Milestones in the First Year

"When you hold your baby in your arms the first time and you think of all the things you can say and do to influence him, it's a tremendous responsibility. What you do can influence not only him, but everyone he meets...for eternity." — Rose Kennedy.

Your baby's first year is a time full of remarkable growth and transformation. For parents, it can be exciting and sometimes overwhelming, as every tiny milestone feels monumental.

This incredible journey touches on *cognitive growth*, *physical milestones*, and *emotional bonding*. These changes don't happen in isolation - they're deeply intertwined, shaping how your baby learns, explores, and connects with the world.

Understanding your baby's development during their first year will help you adapt to their transformation with confidence. So, let's start by taking a closer look at how cognitive, physical, and emotional milestones typically unfold in the first twelve months.

Cognitive Development

During the first year, your baby's brain rapidly develops, creating the foundation for learning, thinking, and interacting with the world. They are constantly absorbing information through their senses and experiences.

One of the most significant cognitive milestones in this period is *object permanence*, which typically emerges around 6-8 months. This is when babies typically start to realize that objects and people still exist, even when they can't see them, and this leads to new behaviors, like searching for hidden toys or expressing anxiety when you leave the room.

Your baby is also improving their ability to focus and track objects. Simple games like peek-a-boo and playing with sensory toys help to stimulate these early cognitive abilities and help them understand their environment. When your baby experiments with actions like dropping toys or banging objects together, they're exploring cause and effect, which is essential for cognitive development.

Physical Development

Your baby's physical development in the first year or so includes gross motor skills, such as rolling over, sitting up, crawling, and eventually pulling themselves to stand. It also includes fine motor skills, which involve hand and finger movements, such as grasping toys. Your baby is born with reflexes that gradually give way to more voluntary actions as their muscles strengthen and neural pathways mature.

Every baby is different, though—some may start crawling at six months, while others might take longer. These variations are normal, and milestones should be seen as guidelines rather than strict timelines.

The same goes for teeth—some babies are sporting their first pearly whites as early as four months, while others might not get their first tooth until well into their first year. Both are perfectly normal, though it can feel like a competition if your neighbor's baby is flashing a toothy grin while yours is still all gums. Rest assured, those tiny teeth will appear when the time is right!

Enjoy the experience of seeing your baby grow and encourage their physical development through safe exploration. Provide tummy time, soft surfaces to move on, and interesting objects within their reach. The American Academy of Pediatrics (2018) emphasizes that giving your baby a safe space to explore helps them build confidence in their abilities and encourages physical growth.

Emotional Development

In their first year, your baby forms an emotional bond with you that will shape their future sense of security.

Emotional development at this stage involves learning to trust and recognizing basic emotional cues. Each time you respond to your baby's needs with warmth and sensitivity, you're fostering a secure attachment, the foundation for their emotional well-being.

Your newborn relies entirely on you to help regulate their emotions, whether by soothing them when they cry or creating a calming bedtime routine. Your baby will begin to express joy through smiles and laughter and seek comfort through cuddles. They may also show frustration or distress when they feel uncomfortable or upset.

As you learn to interpret your baby's unique emotional cues— including different cries for hunger or discomfort— you'll be able to respond more effectively, strengthening your bonds of love and trust.

Of course, you won't get it right every time, but that's perfectly fine. As child psychologist Mary Ainsworth noted, "it is not the frequency of moments of attunement but their quality and consistency that matters most". In other words, what matters is that you're there, present, and tuned in, helping your baby feel safe and secure.

Your main responsibilities are to offer assistance, motivation, and affection as your little one goes through these stages at their speed. Instead of fixating on whether your child's reaching each milestone "on schedule", take joy in their unique advancements and understand that your support and nurturing play the biggest roles in their growth and progress.

Building Trust, Bonding, and Communication

"It was the tiniest thing I ever decided to put my whole life into." — Terri Guillemets.

Gentle parenting is all about recognizing that even at this young age, your baby is a tiny human with emotions, needs, and the capacity to communicate—just not with words yet! So, in the first year of your baby's life, the focus is on building a foundation of trust and connection by being responsive, present, and gentle in your interactions.

This approach encourages you to see your baby as a whole person with emotions and needs, from the moment they emerge into the world. By creating a secure, loving environment and staying attuned to your baby's cues, you're laying the foundation for a lifelong bond and nurturing your baby's emotional and social development.

Consistency and Responsiveness

At this stage, your baby is learning to trust you based on how consistently you respond to their needs. When they cry, they're not trying to manipulate you—they're signaling that they need something, whether it's comfort, food, or just a reassuring touch.

The gentle parenting approach emphasizes responding with empathy, as it helps your baby develop a secure attachment and feel safe in their new world.

Psychologist Erik Erikson proposed that during their first year, babies go through what he called the *trust versus mistrust* stage (Erikson, 1950). If their needs are met consistently and lovingly, they learn to trust you and the world around them.

Of course, you shouldn't feel pressured to respond perfectly, every time; gentle parenting recognizes that you won't always get it right. What matters most is that you aim to be consistently present and attuned to your baby's cues - while being gentle and non-judgemental to yourself.

One way to build trust is to establish routines that give your baby a sense of predictability. For example, creating a calming bedtime routine or having a consistent feeding schedule can help your baby know what to expect and feel secure. Routines need to be practical and adapted to the rhythms of your household, so there's no need to be rigid—just create some simple and comforting patterns that help your baby make sense of their day.

Creating a Strong Emotional Connection

> *"You are my sun, my moon, and all of my stars."*
> — E. E. Cummings.

Bonding is not just about holding your baby; it's about the quality of your interactions. Holding your baby skin-to-skin, maintaining eye contact, and using a soothing voice can all create a powerful bond. These moments of physical closeness help your baby feel secure and connected and form the basis for a secure attachment.

Studies have shown that touch has numerous benefits, from reducing stress and promoting better sleep to supporting physical growth and cognitive development.

Responsive touch, such as cuddling, gentle rocking, and massaging is a powerful way to strengthen the bond between you and your baby. Another aspect of bonding is simply being present. Your baby is sensitive to your emotions and responses, so being calm, attentive, and present sends a powerful message of love and security.

Bonding is a two-way street, though. It's not just about what you do for your baby, but also about how you experience this connection. Take time to savor the small moments, like the first smile or the way your baby gazes up at you during feeding, and feel the unique and profound joy of being a parent.

Laying the Groundwork for Emotional Development

Your baby may not have words yet, but they're already communicating with you. Gentle parenting emphasizes listening and responding to these early cues—whether it's a coo, a cry, or the way your baby turns toward your voice. Your interaction helps your baby feel heard and understood, laying the groundwork for healthy emotional development.

By responding promptly and gently to your baby's signals, you're letting them know that their feelings matter. Over time, this creates a secure environment where they feel comfortable expressing their needs. Even simple actions, like making eye contact, imitating your baby's sounds, or using a soothing voice, reinforce their attempts at communication and help them understand that you're there to help.

Renowned pediatrician, Dr. T. Berry Brazelton, described these early exchanges as a *"dance" between parent and baby*, where each response builds trust and mutual understanding. As your baby grows, they'll start to recognize the give-and-take of communication, which will be essential for developing empathy and emotional regulation later on.

Ideas for Building Trust, Bonding, and Communication

> "All those clichés, those things you hear about having a baby and motherhood—all of them are true. And all of them are the most beautiful things you will ever experience." — Penelope Cruz.

To sum up, here are a few practical gentle parenting tips to help strengthen your bond, build trust, and encourage early communication.

Respond with Empathy

When your baby cries, take a moment to consider what they might need. Is it a dirty diaper, hunger, or just the need for comfort? Sometimes, it's a matter of trial and error until you realize what they are trying to tell you. Responding with empathy doesn't imply that you'll be able to solve everything instantly—it's about being present and showing your baby that their feelings matter.

Practice Skin-to-Skin Contact

Hold your baby close as much as possible, especially in the early months. The warmth and skin-to-skin contact can help regulate your baby's heartbeat, reduce stress levels, and promote bonding. But this isn't just for moms—dads, grandparents, and other caregivers can participate too, so encourage them to share these wonderful moments of connection.

Use a Gentle Voice

Speak softly and positively to your baby, even when they're too young to understand your words. Let your tone convey love, safety, and warmth to help your baby feel secure. Narrate your actions ("Now I'm going to change your diaper") or describe what your baby is doing ("You're looking so curious at that toy"). By narrating your actions, you capture your baby's attention and keep them engaged. This practice helps them develop their listening skills and understand the importance of paying attention in social situations.

- **Maintain Eye Contact and Smile**. Babies are drawn to faces, and maintaining eye contact while smiling reassures them and encourages early social interaction. These simple moments of connection are powerful bonding tools.

- **Imitate Your Baby's Sounds**. When your baby starts cooing or babbling, mimic their sounds and engage in a "conversation." This helps them understand the rhythm of communication and reinforces their efforts to convey what they want.

Again, let me say it. there's no perfect way to bond or communicate with your baby. The key is to stay present and respond with empathy. Every interaction is an opportunity to deepen your connection and help your baby feel loved and understood, so trust your instincts and you'll develop your own style as you go along.

Creating an Environment for Exploration & Skills

In the first year of your baby's life, creating a nurturing and thoughtfully designed environment is essential for supporting exploration, building confidence, and encouraging early independence. The Montessori approach emphasizes respecting even the youngest child's natural curiosity by offering freedom within limits and providing developmentally appropriate opportunities to practice new skills.

Preparing a Montessori-Style Space

One of the foundational concepts of Montessori philosophy is that of a "prepared environment". It's about thoughtfully arranging your home to support your baby's independence, movement, and sense of discovery. In the first year, a prepared environment doesn't have to be elaborate—it's about ensuring your baby has safe spaces and the right tools to explore at their own pace.

Create a Montessori-inspired space by setting up a little "yes zone" for your baby—a safe place where they can explore without you constantly saying, "No!" This simple approach makes life easier for both of you and encourages your baby's natural curiosity.

A simple floor bed instead of a crib, for example, offers your baby the freedom to move and explore when they wake up. Baby-proofed low shelves filled with age-appropriate toys and books allow them to reach and select items on their own. Soft mats on the floor provide a safe place for tummy time, crawling, and, eventually walking.

Instead of a playpen, we often laid a soft rug in the living room with a few toys within reach. Watching my baby discover new textures and sounds made me realize exploration doesn't require fancy equipment. It's about creating a space that invites them to learn safely.

Aim to create an environment that is both beautiful and uncluttered. This doesn't imply expensive remodeling; instead, it's about being intentional with your baby's surroundings.

For example, put out only a few toys or books at a time to avoid overwhelming your baby, and rotate them regularly to spark fresh interest. Decorating spaces with bright colors or imaginative themes can add to the sensory experience, making the space inviting and stimulating without excess.

Maria Montessori explained, "The environment must be rich in motives which lend interest to activity and invite the child to conduct his own experiences." By setting up spaces designed for self-directed exploration, you're sending a powerful message to your baby that will build their confidence. 'You are capable and trusted to explore this world'.

Building Skills and Independence, One Step at a Time

In the first year, your baby is constantly learning about their body, surroundings, and how to interact with the world. This is an ideal time to gently encourage real-life skills that foster their confidence and independence. For example.

- **Reaching and Grasping**. Instead of handing your baby a toy, place it just within their reach, encouraging them to extend their arm and grasp it themselves. This builds both motor skills and problem-solving abilities.

- **Introducing Self-Feeding**. Around six months, many babies show readiness to start exploring solid foods. The Montessori approach recommends allowing your baby to experiment with picking up soft, bite-sized foods with their fingers, and as they become more adept, give them baby utensils such as a fork and spoon. It's messy, yes, but it supports their independence and the development of fine motor skills.

- **Non-Assisted Movement**. If your baby is beginning to sit or crawl, you might notice they want to explore on their own. Instead of rushing in to help at every moment, offer gentle encouragement and space to try things for themselves. Montessori emphasized this principle, writing, "Never help a child with a task at which he feels he can succeed." When you step back and let your baby try, you're helping them to grow in self-reliance and determination.

How This Builds Confidence and Emotional Security

When you let your baby take the lead in small, achievable ways, they're not just learning new skills; they're learning to trust themselves. This sense of accomplishment fosters a deep-rooted confidence that stays with them as they grow. Every time your baby successfully reaches a toy or picks up a piece of food, they're having a mini-celebration of their capabilities.

This approach also helps you see and celebrate everyday victories. It shifts your focus from doing everything for your baby to supporting their growth—one small step at a time.

Practical Tips for a Montessori-Inspired First Year

- **Create Safe Exploration Zones**. Set up an attractive, uncluttered, baby-proofed area where your baby can explore freely, without constant intervention. Use low shelves, soft rugs, and accessible toys that encourage independent play.

- **Offer Real-World Experiences**. From holding a soft spoon during mealtime to letting your baby explore the textures of different fabrics, small everyday moments provide rich learning opportunities.

- **Encourage Movement and Observation**. Allow your baby to watch you as you go about your day, and occasionally describe your actions. Whether you're folding laundry or preparing food, these small observations contribute to their understanding of the world.

Ultimately, combining a prepared environment with gentle parenting principles allows you to support your baby in their natural drive to explore, build skills, and grow in confidence.

Remember, this first year is not about pushing your baby to meet milestones faster or expecting them to be independent in ways they're not ready for. It's about creating a loving and responsive environment that honors your baby's need for exploration and connection.

Practical Ideas for Peaceful Sleep

"If I'm forced to work a 24-hour shift, I'm sure glad this little thing is my boss." — Anon.

The first year with your baby is full of rapid changes, new experiences, and countless learning moments. While gentle parenting with a Montessori twist provides a guiding philosophy, the day-to-day reality often revolves around meeting your baby's most basic needs—sleep, nourishment, and play. Let's start by exploring some practical strategies for sleep, so you can create a loving and peaceful environment for your baby - and yourself.

Supporting Healthy Sleep Patterns

> *"A mother's arms are made of tenderness, and children sleep soundly in them."* — *Victor Hugo.*

Sleep is a significant focus and concern for new parents. It can also be one of the most challenging aspects to navigate. Gentle parenting emphasizes responding to your baby's cues and creating a sense of safety and trust, even during sleep routines. Here's a breakdown of strategies for different stages of the first year.

First Six Weeks. Nurturing Newborn Sleep

In the first six weeks, newborns need to eat every 2-4 hours, which means their sleep patterns are fragmented and often unpredictable. They spend most of their time alternating between feeding and sleeping, with brief moments of alertness.

During this stage.

- **Follow Your Baby's Cues.** Newborns show early signs of sleepiness such as yawning, staring off, or fussing. Respond promptly to these cues to prevent them from becoming overtired.

- **Accept Frequent Night Wakings.** It's normal for newborns to wake every few hours for feeding. Embrace this phase as an essential part of growth and bonding, and try to rest when your baby sleeps to recharge.

- **Safe Sleep Practices.** Ensure a safe sleep environment by placing your baby on their back on a firm mattress with no loose bedding or toys. A swaddle can provide comfort by mimicking the snugness of the womb, but make sure it's not too tight and discontinue use when they start showing signs of rolling over.

3 to 6 Months. Establishing Sleep Patterns

Between 3 and 6 months, babies begin to consolidate their sleep and may start to develop longer nighttime stretches. This is a period when routines can help.

- **Create a Consistent Routine.** Establish a predictable bedtime routine that signals winding down. This can include a warm bath, a gentle massage, singing a lullaby, or reading a soft story. This routine helps cue your baby that sleep time is approaching.

- **Day-Night Differentiation.** Reinforce the difference between day and night by keeping daytime interactions lively and night wakings calm and quiet. This helps your baby gradually understand that nighttime is for sleeping.

- **Support Self-Soothing.** At this stage, babies may begin to develop self-soothing habits such as sucking their thumb or rubbing a soft blanket. Support this development by allowing brief moments for your baby to settle themselves before intervening.

6 to 12 Months. Building Sleep Independence

By 6 months to a year, many babies can sleep longer stretches and may only need one or two night-feedings, if any. However, teething and developmental milestones can disrupt sleep, so.

- **Maintain a Flexible Routine.** Continue with your established bedtime routine, adapting it as your baby grows. Follow a predictable pattern to provide reassurance and help signal that it's time to sleep.

- **Respond with Gentle Reassurance.** Night wakings are still normal during this stage, especially during teething or growth spurts. Assess whether your baby needs comfort or is simply transitioning through sleep cycles. If they need attention, respond calmly and keep interactions minimal to avoid fully waking them.

- **Adjust Nap Schedules.** Your baby's daytime sleep needs will evolve during this period, often moving from multiple short naps to fewer, longer ones. Watch for signs of overtiredness, such as crankiness or rubbing eyes, and adjust naps accordingly to help maintain nighttime sleep quality.

Should I Sleep With My Baby?

Co-sleeping, or sharing a bed with your baby, is a topic that often comes up for new parents. For some, it feels like a natural choice that fosters closeness and makes nighttime feeding easier. It seems like a natural extension of a gentle parenting approach. For others, safety concerns and the impact on their own sleep patterns weigh heavily on their decision. It's an important topic , and advice varies widely depending on the source.

Is Co-Sleeping Safe?

Many pediatricians and child safety organizations, including the American Academy of Pediatrics (AAP), advise against co-sleeping due to safety risks including suffocation, overheating, or the baby accidentally falling from the bed. The AAP recommends a safer alternative. room-sharing without bed-sharing. This means having your baby sleep in the same room as you, but in their own sleep space, such as a bassinet or crib, to reduce the risk of Sudden Infant Death Syndrome (SIDS).

Benefits of Co-Sleeping

Co-sleeping advocates, including some pediatric sleep consultants, highlight benefits such as easier breastfeeding, stronger parent-child bonding, and potentially more restful nights for parents and babies. For breastfeeding mothers in particular, co-sleeping can make night wakings less disruptive. It can also align with cultural practices that emphasize physical closeness between parent and child, offering emotional comfort to both.

Consider the Impact on Parental Sleep

While co-sleeping can make breastfeeding more convenient, it's worth considering its impact on your own sleep. Some parents find that sharing a bed with their baby leads to fragmented or lighter sleep due to their awareness of the baby's movements and sounds. For others, co-sleeping brings peace of mind and promotes better rest. Every family is different, so it's important to evaluate how co-sleeping affects your physical and mental well-being.

Safe Co-Sleeping Guidelines

If you decide co-sleeping is the right choice for your family, it's essential to follow current safety guidelines to reduce risks.

- Use a firm mattress, and avoid soft bedding, pillows, or comforters that could pose a suffocation risk.

- Ensure the baby cannot fall from the bed.

- Avoid co-sleeping if either parent has consumed alcohol, is under the influence of medication, or is excessively fatigued.

- Keep the sleep area clear of toys, pets, or any other potential hazards.

Transitioning Gradually

If co-sleeping works for your family but you're ready to transition your baby to independent sleep, this can be done gradually. Start by having your baby sleep in a bassinet beside your bed, and over time, move them to their own crib or room.

Ultimately, deciding whether to co-sleep should be based on what feels right for your family while considering your baby's safety and your own rest. If you're unsure or have concerns, consult your pediatrician to obtain updated advice and guidance that fits your unique circumstances.

Helpful Sleeping Tips for All Stages

Create a Calm, Clutter-Free Sleep Space

While it's tempting to add lots of decorations and toys, a peaceful, uncluttered sleep environment supports better rest. A simple, cozy setup with minimal visual stimulation helps keep your baby relaxed.

Stay Responsive

Gentle parenting encourages listening to your baby's needs, whether through quick reassurance or helping them settle back down. This approach builds trust and ensures that your baby feels safe and secure.

Be Flexible

When it comes to your baby's sleep, be flexible. Growth spurts, teething, colds, or other changes can temporarily disrupt their routine. During these times, focus on addressing what you can— whether that's soothing the discomfort of teething or giving extra cuddles during an illness. Once the challenging period passes, gently guide your baby back into their usual rhythm.

A consistent yet adaptable approach helps your baby feel supported while maintaining healthy sleep habits over time.

Mealtimes that Encourage Sensory Exploration and Independence

> "What good mothers and fathers instinctively feel like doing for their babies is usually best after all."
> — Benjamin Spock.

Feeding is another essential area where you can combine gentle parenting and Montessori principles. Whether you're breastfeeding, bottle-feeding, or starting to introduce solid foods, the goal is to foster a nourishing and connected experience.

Make Mealtimes a Calm and Connected Experience

When feeding your baby, slow down and create moments of connection. Hold eye contact, smile, and talk softly to them. Whether breastfeeding, bottle-feeding, or spoon-feeding, these interactions reinforce trust and bonding.

Introduce Self-Feeding and Exploration

As your baby shows readiness for solid foods - typically from around 6 months - offer opportunities for self-feeding. Montessori encourages babies to explore food textures, practice picking up small pieces, and even hold a soft spoon. Remember, early mealtime experiences are not just about nourishment; they're about exploration and skill-building.

Responsive Feeding

Pay close attention to your baby's hunger and fullness cues. Avoid pressuring them to finish a bottle or a bowl of food. Instead, trust that your baby knows when they're full. Responsive feeding is a cornerstone of both gentle parenting and the Montessori approach, encouraging autonomy and mutual respect from the start.

Gentle Play to Stimulate the Senses

Playtime is your baby's first chance to explore, experiment, and learn about the world. Both gentle parenting and Montessori emphasize respectful interactions and provide opportunities for independent discovery. Here are a few ideas.

Offer Simple, Open-Ended Toys

In the first year, focus on toys that engage your baby's senses and encourage exploration. Soft blocks, rattles, simple stacking rings, and textured fabrics are excellent choices. Rotate toys every few days to keep things fresh. You don't need a lot—just a few engaging items that spark curiosity.

Encourage Movement and Exploration

Babies are naturally curious and eager to move. Create a safe play space where your baby can freely roll, crawl, and explore. Low mirrors, soft climbing cushions, or low shelves with easy-to-reach objects provide motivation and support physical development.

Narrate and Engage

Talk to your baby during playtime, describing what they're doing and seeing. "You found the red block! What does it feel like?" This form of responsive interaction not only builds language skills but also strengthens your bond.

Incorporate Real-Life Skills in Play

Even simple activities like pouring water from a small jug into a cup or using a soft cloth to wipe a table introduce life skills in a playful, enjoyable way. Maria Montessori emphasized that children are naturally inclined to imitate adults and learn through real-life experiences. "Children acquire knowledge through experience in the environment."

Fun Play Ideas for the First Year

Tummy Time with Sensory Mats

Tummy time strengthens the neck, shoulder, and core muscles, laying the foundation for crawling and sitting. Incorporating sensory mats enhances this activity by stimulating your baby's sense of touch and curiosity.

How to Play.

- Place your baby on a mat with different textures, such as soft fleece, crinkly fabric, and smooth plastic sections.
- Scatter high-contrast toys or patterned cards around the mat to encourage visual engagement.
- Add small fabric tags or loops for grasping to support fine motor development.

- Lie down next to your baby to offer encouragement and model interaction with the textures.

Variation. Use a rolled towel under your baby's chest if they're reluctant to stay on their tummy, making it easier for them to lift their head.

Water Play with Gentle Splashing

Water play provides tactile stimulation and introduces the concept of cause and effect, such as seeing ripples form when they splash.

How to Play.

- Fill a shallow basin or baby bath with warm water, adding a few floating toys for visual interest.

- Let your baby gently touch and splash the water with their hands and feet, feeling the sensation of movement.

- Use a small cup to trickle water over their hands, feet, or belly, narrating what's happening to build language connections.

- For an added sensory element, place a damp washcloth or sponge in the water for squeezing and patting.

Always supervise water play closely, and ensure the water level is shallow and safe.

Soft Fabric Basket Exploration

Exploring different textures helps babies develop their sense of touch and improve hand-eye coordination.

How to Play.

- Fill a shallow basket with small swatches of fabric (e.g., silk, cotton, fleece, and satin) in various colors and patterns.

- Encourage your baby to grasp, pull, and feel the fabrics, talking about the textures as they explore (e.g., "This one is so soft! This one is crinkly!").

- Tie knots in some fabrics to add interest or hide a small toy beneath a piece for your baby to "find."

- As they grow, you can introduce fabrics that make sounds, like crinkly paper or ribbons with bells attached.

Mirrored Play

Mirrors help babies develop visual tracking, self-awareness, and early social understanding as they begin recognizing their reflection.

How to Play.

- Prop a baby-safe mirror at floor level during tummy time. Watch as your baby lifts their head to look at their reflection.

- Sit your baby in your lap facing a mirror and make funny faces, encouraging them to mimic your expressions.

- Point out features in the reflection, such as "There's your nose!" or "Look at your big smile!"

- Use a hand-held mirror to catch your baby's gaze while gently moving it from side to side for visual tracking practice.

Peekaboo with a Scarf

This helps develop object permanence and builds anticipation and joy.

- **How to Play.** Hide your face behind a lightweight scarf, then reveal yourself with a cheerful "Peekaboo!" Let your baby take turns holding or moving the scarf.

Rolling Ball Chase

Encourages reaching, grasping, and early crawling movements.

- **How to Play.** Roll a soft, lightweight ball slightly out of your baby's reach during tummy time. Encourage them to reach or wiggle towards it.

Discovering the Big, Beautiful World

Babies are natural explorers, and introducing them to the world outside their immediate surroundings provides countless opportunities for sensory stimulation and cognitive development. Whether venturing into nature or visiting cultural spots, these activities can spark curiosity and lay the foundation for a lifelong love of discovery.

Nature Walks in a Stroller or Carrier

Fresh air and the soothing rhythm of movement can be calming for babies while offering exposure to the sights, sounds, and textures of nature. Hearing birds chirp, seeing leaves flutter, and feeling a gentle breeze stimulate their developing senses.

Enrich the Walk.

- Narrate your walk. "Look at those green leaves!" or "Can you hear the rustling wind?" helps build early language skills.

- Let your baby touch safe objects like smooth stones, soft grass, or tree bark to explore new textures.

- Pause under trees to let them watch the light filtering through leaves to encourage visual tracking.

Tip. Choose quieter trails or parks to minimize overstimulation and maximize connection with nature.

A Trip to the Botanical Garden

Botanical gardens introduce a variety of scents, colors, and textures in a tranquil setting. Babies absorb these experiences while you enjoy the tranquil atmosphere and moments of calm.

What to Do.

- Guide your baby's attention to vibrant flowers, the scent of herbs, or the sound of a bubbling fountain.

- Encourage them to gently touch non-toxic plants or feel the texture of a smooth leaf.

- Talk about what you're experiencing together. "These flowers are bright red—look how they sway in the breeze!"

Exploring a Baby-Friendly Museum or Art Exhibit

Museums and art exhibits offer visually stimulating environments with contrasting colors, shapes, and patterns that capture a baby's attention.

What to Do.

- Visit sections with large, colorful artwork or interactive displays designed for families.

- Pause in front of exhibits with bold patterns or simple shapes and encourage your baby to observe.

- Narrate your experience. "Look at this big, blue painting—it's so smooth and bright!"

Check ahead for baby-friendly facilities and quieter times to visit.

An Aquarium Adventure

Watching fish glide through the water and observing vibrant underwater scenes provides a multisensory experience that captivates babies. The gentle lighting and soothing sounds are especially calming.

What to Do.

- Hold your baby close to tanks where they can watch the movement of fish and other sea creatures.

- Encourage them to track the movement of brightly colored fish or large, slow-moving creatures like turtles.

- Talk about what you see, emphasizing motion and color. "See the yellow fish swimming fast? Now it's hiding behind the coral!"

Look for aquariums with dedicated toddler or family areas and visit on days that are quieter and less crowded.

Helping Your Baby Develop Their Vision Through Play

Your baby's vision develops rapidly in the first year, transforming from blurry shapes to more detailed and colorful images. Understanding these changes can help you provide the right visual stimulation to support their growth.

Babies Love High-Contrast Patterns!

At birth, a baby's eyesight is limited and blurry, with a focus range of just 8-12 inches. During the first few months, they can only clearly see high-contrast colors like black, white, and red. Patterns in these colors are easier for them to focus on, as their ability to distinguish finer details is still maturing.

Stimulation of Visual Development

High-contrast patterns provide the ideal stimuli for a newborn's developing brain. These visuals engage the visual system, helping babies strengthen their ability to track objects with their eyes, recognize shapes, and develop hand-eye coordination.

Enhanced Contrast Recognition

Babies naturally perceive contrasting colors much better than subtle differences in shades. Bold designs with clear distinctions between light and dark are captivating and help their visual and cognitive systems grow.

How Vision Changes Over Time

0-6 Months

- **Newborn to 2 Months**. Babies are most fascinated by black-and-white patterns. During this stage, their visual world is limited to simple contrasts, as they cannot yet focus on subtle or complex designs.

- **2-4 Months**. As visual acuity improves, babies begin tracking objects more smoothly and can follow simple black-and-white patterns.

- **5-6 Months**. Babies start seeing a broader range of colors and show interest in more complex visuals. However, high-contrast designs remain engaging as their vision continues to mature.

Practical Ways to Support Visual Development

Black Marker on White Paper Plates

A simple design on a paper plate is an effective way to stimulate your baby's vision. The stark contrast between black and white is visually engaging, while the large plate provides an easy target for your baby to focus on. Draw bold patterns like spirals or stripes, and position them where your baby can see and reach.

Other High-Contrast Items

- Books or cards with black-and-white designs
- Simple toys with bold patterns
- DIY patterns using black tape on white surfaces

By introducing high-contrast visuals during these early months, you can help your baby develop stronger visual and cognitive skills, laying the foundation for future learning.

Navigating Typical First-Year Challenges

The first year of your child's life is full of joy and excitement, but even the most prepared parents find themselves facing unexpected situations. The most frequently encountered struggles tend to revolve around sleep and feeding. Calming your baby when they cry persistently and inconsolably can also challenge your confidence in your ability as a parent.

And during this time, maintaining your relationship with your partner after the tsunami of change that your little one, no matter how loved, has created in your lifestyle can also be an aspect of parenting that you hadn't been prepared to face.

So in this section we'll offer some ideas to help you navigate these challenges, maintaining the gentle parenting mindset while keeping your own well-being in mind.

Managing Sleep Deprivation

It's no secret that sleepless nights are part of parenting an infant, and everyone will be happy to share their stories of endless periods of interrupted rest, and days when they moved through life like exhausted zombies.

Some babies may sleep perfectly through the night, but most don't. While there's no perfect solution to this challenge, gentle parenting encourages you to prioritize both your baby's needs and your own mental health.

Share the Load

If you have a partner, take turns with night wakings or set up shifts so each of you can get a longer stretch of rest. Even if you're breastfeeding, it can help if your partner changes diapers or comforts your baby back to sleep. If you take on the feeding duties at night, perhaps if your partner has a tight work schedule, work out when they can take over at other times, so you can have a peaceful and much needed nap.

Nap When You Can

It's a classic piece of advice, but it's essential to rest when your baby sleeps if you can. Even short naps can help recharge you, and lowering your expectations for household chores during these early months can make this more achievable. Practicing short Non Sleep Deep Rest (NSDR) sessions, even for 15 or 20 minutes, can help you restore your energy.

Practice Gentle Self-Compassion

Human beings sleep for a reason, so stay mindful of how challenging sleep deprivation can be. If you're exhausted and feeling irritable or overwhelmed, remember that this is 100% to be expected. and remind yourself that you're doing your best. You might also consider brief moments of mindfulness or deep breathing to help you reset.

Establish Calming Bedtime Routines for Yourself

Just as routines are helpful for your baby, they're also beneficial for you. Even a short bedtime ritual—like dimming the lights, taking a warm shower, or listening to soothing music—can help prepare your body for sleep and signal to your brain that it's time to wind down.

Navigating Feeding Struggles

Feeding your baby is one of the most intimate and emotionally charged aspects of parenting, and new mothers often feel immense pressure to "get it right." For many, this pressure is tied to breastfeeding, which is commonly seen as the ideal way to nourish a baby. However, breastfeeding isn't always straightforward, and life's demands can complicate the best-laid plans.

Acknowledging the Pressure to Breastfeed

Society often idealizes breastfeeding as the ultimate mark of good parenting. This can leave new mothers feeling intense guilt or frustration if they encounter difficulties. While breastfeeding is natural, it's not always easy. Issues like latching problems, low milk supply, or the physical discomfort of nursing can leave mothers feeling inadequate or discouraged.

External Challenges and Stigma

Beyond the physical challenges, public perceptions and limited facilities for breastfeeding can make mothers feel unwelcome in many spaces. Nursing in public can be uncomfortable or stigmatized, leading to feelings of isolation. Some workplaces may lack appropriate accommodations, making it difficult to pump milk regularly, which adds further stress for working parents.

Breaking the Stigma Around Bottle Feeding

For mothers who choose or need to bottle feed, there's often a sense of judgment or inadequacy - real or perceived. Whether due to medical reasons, supply issues, or personal preference, opting for formula or a combination of feeding methods should be a valid choice without stigma. Gentle parenting advocates being kind to yourself and making feeding decisions that prioritize the well-being of your baby and your family over the judgements of others..

Responsive Feeding as a Gentle Approach

Instead of focusing solely on how a baby is fed, responsive feeding emphasizes being attuned to your baby's cues, whether you're breastfeeding or bottle-feeding. It involves looking out for signs of hunger and fullness and responding to your baby's needs, and can free you from the pressure of trying to hit arbitrary feeding 'milestones.'

Embrace Flexibility

Trusting yourself and making decisions based on what works for you and your baby is the cornerstone of a gentle parenting mindset. Feeding is not a one-size-fits-all scenario. Some parents find success with mixed feeding (both breastfeeding and formula), while others rely entirely on breast- or bottle-feeding. Trust your instinct and do what feels right for your baby and family - without guilt. .

Seek Support Without Judgment

Be gentle with yourself and reach out for support rather than struggling alone, as this can be vital for your mental health as well as your baby's feeding success. Don't hesitate to focus on your well-being as a parent, just as much as you do on your baby's, because your emotional health and confidence are central to building a loving connection with your child.

Seek out environments where support and guidance come without judgment. If you're struggling with breastfeeding, consider reaching out to a lactation consultant or a supportive community of other parents who've been in your situation. By being responsive and flexible, and letting go of external pressures, you can create a feeding experience that nurtures not only your baby but also yourself.

Introduce Solids with Curiosity and Patience

When your baby is ready for solids, approach this development with patience and curiosity. Offer them a variety of textures and flavors, and let your baby explore them at their own pace. Gentle parenting and Montessori principles both emphasize that early eating experiences should be joyful and exploratory, rather than rushed or pressured. And yes, they will be messy - toddler parents tend to have particular challenges cleaning up foods such as rice, peanut butter, and oatmeal, which sets like a special blend of concrete mixed with added glue - and that's where patience comes in.

Comforting Your Crying Baby

> *"When your baby cries, think of it as their way of saying, "I need you." Your calm presence is more powerful than any 'perfect' parenting strategy."*

When your baby cries persistently despite being fed, rested, and clean It can feel overwhelming In newborns this phase is often referred to as the "fourth trimester," as it's a period of adjustment for your baby as they adapt to life outside the womb. A gentle parenting approach focuses on empathy, understanding, and practical strategies to soothe your little one while maintaining a calm and nurturing environment.

First Step. Check for Common Discomforts

Even when basic needs seem met, small discomforts can upset a baby.

- **Gas or Colic Relief.** Gently pat or rub your baby's back to encourage burping, or use "bicycle legs" to help relieve trapped gas. Specialized anti-colic bottles or gripe water may also help if recommended by your pediatrician.

- **Temperature Check.** Ensure your baby isn't too hot or cold by feeling their neck or chest, as extremities can sometimes feel cooler.

- **Wet Diaper.** Even if recently changed, a quick diaper check may solve the crying.

Tip. Babies can't yet communicate discomfort, so systematically checking these common causes often provides relief.

Try the 5 S's by Dr. Harvey Karp

Some parents find Dr. Karp's five-step method is helpful. It mimics the comforting environment of the womb, triggering a calming reflex.

- **Swaddle.** Wrap your baby snugly to provide a sense of security.

- **Side or Stomach Position.** Hold your baby on their side or stomach (always supervised) to ease discomfort.

- **Shushing Sounds.** A gentle "shhh" mimics the soothing sounds of the womb.

- **Swinging or Rocking.** Rhythmic, gentle motion can help calm your baby.

- **Sucking.** Offer a pacifier or let your baby nurse for comfort.

Tip. Swaddling and shushing often work best when combined, especially during the evening hours when babies are more likely to cry.

Comfort Them with Gentle Motion

Babies find rhythmic motion calming as it mirrors the sensations they experienced in the womb.

- **Rocking and Swaying.** Hold your baby close and gently rock or sway, either in your arms, a glider, or a baby carrier.

- **Babywearing.** Using a sling or wrap can offer your baby warmth and closeness while leaving your hands free.

- **Car Rides or Stroller Walks.** The movement can lull them into a calmer state.

Research Insight. Studies have shown that motion stimulates the vestibular system, which helps activate a baby's calming reflex.

Embrace Skin-to-Skin Contact

Holding your baby skin-to-skin not only comforts them but also provides physiological benefits.

- **How It Works.** Your baby feels your heartbeat, warmth, and steady breathing, which help regulate their stress levels and reduce crying.

- **When to Use.** This method is especially effective during fussy periods or after feeding.

Tip. Skin-to-skin can be done by either parent, fostering bonding and calming even the most unsettled baby.

Create a Soothing Environment

Adjusting your surroundings to reduce stimulation can have a calming effect.

- **Dim Lights.** Babies are highly sensitive to bright lights, so a softly lit room can help signal rest time.

- **White Noise or Gentle Music.** These sounds mimic the womb and help mask external noises that might startle your baby.

- **Warm Bath.** A brief, warm bath can relax your baby and set the stage for a more peaceful evening.

Tip. Combine these elements into a consistent bedtime routine to help your baby recognize the transition to sleep.

Keep Yourself Calm and Centered

Babies are incredibly attuned to their parents' emotions. If you're feeling frustrated or overwhelmed, take a moment to breathe deeply and reset. It's okay to set your baby down in a safe space, like a crib, while you take a short break to recharge.

When to Seek Help

However, if your baby's crying persists despite your best efforts, or if they show signs of illness (fever, difficulty breathing, or sudden changes in behavior), consult your pediatrician. Persistent colic or reflux may also require professional advice.

By responding with empathy and calm, you're not just soothing your baby but also building a foundation of trust and security. These moments, while challenging, are opportunities to strengthen your bond and deepen your understanding of your baby's unique needs.

Supporting Your Baby's Bond with Your Partner

In the first year, it's easy to become entirely focused on your baby's needs and overlook the other 'significant other' in your child's life. Supporting your baby's bond with your partner not only enriches your baby's life but also strengthens your connection as a couple.

Encourage Active Involvement

One way to foster a strong bond between your baby and your partner is to encourage hands-on involvement. Invite your partner to participate in activities like diaper changes, bath time, or baby massage.Be ready to stand back and let your partner have moments to bond on their own without stepping in to guide or "correct" them.

Communicate Openly

Parenting together can sometimes feel like navigating uncharted territory, and it's normal for disagreements to arise - especially when one or both of you is cranky due to sleep deprivation. Open and compassionate communication about your expectations, concerns, and emotional needs can help you both feel heard and supported. Maintaining a united front in your parenting approach is more about being flexible together than always agreeing on every detail.

Celebrate Your Partner's Wins

Take the time to appreciate each other's contributions, even the small ones. Compliment your partner when you notice them being patient, or express gratitude when they take over for a bit to let you rest. Acknowledging each other's efforts goes a long way in fostering a positive partnership. (More about this in Chapter 6).

Enriching Your Relationship as a Couple

During this demanding first year, it's normal for your relationship with your partner to feel stretched thin. However, as part of your gentle parenting approach ensure that you are not neglecting each other or your relationship. Be open about how you want to support each other as your life transitions to the stage where your new focus is on nurturing the life you have brought into the world

- **Plan Simple Connection Moments**. A 'date night' doesn't have to be elaborate. Simply setting aside time to have a quiet dinner at home after the baby is asleep, or taking a walk together with the stroller, can create meaningful connection points. Use these moments to reconnect, laugh, and check in with each other.

- **Be Gentle with Each Other's Emotions**. Remember what you first loved about the other and keep in mind that both of you are likely adjusting to your new roles and pressures. Gentle parenting isn't just about how you treat your child—it extends to how you treat each other. Approach your partner with empathy, listen with patience, and forgive each other's mistakes along the way.

Finding Your Balance in the First Year

Parenting an infant is no easy task, and the challenges you face—including sleep deprivation, feeding struggles, and maintaining your connection with your partner—are all part of a shared experience many parents go through.

Parenting isn't about perfection; it's about presence. On tough days, remember. your baby doesn't need a flawless parent—they need you. Trust yourself and take it one moment at a time.

If you're worried or feeling overwhelmed, know this—every parent feels like this sometimes. Celebrate small wins, forgive yourself, and keep going. You're already doing the most important thing - loving your baby.

Take comfort in knowing that gentle parenting allows space for imperfection, adaptation, and learning together as a family. You don't have to do everything perfectly; you just have to be present and willing to grow.

Remember. You ARE Enough!

The first year of your baby's life is filled with constant change, not just for them but for you as well. As you navigate sleep, nourishment, and play, it's important to embrace the fact that every baby is unique. What works for one child may not work for another, and that's okay.

Gentle parenting and Montessori principles both emphasize the importance of regarding your baby as an individual. Gentle parenting encourages flexibility and emotional responsiveness, helping you attune to your baby's needs. This might mean adjusting your feeding routine when they hit a growth spurt, changing their sleep environment as they develop new patterns, or simplifying playtime when they seem overwhelmed. By staying present and attuned, you create a foundation of trust and security.

Montessori's focus on respecting the child complements this beautifully. In the first year, this means creating opportunities for your baby to engage at their own pace, fostering independence even in small ways. For example, offering them a chance to hold a spoon during mealtime or explore a toy during play encourages problem-solving and a sense of agency. Respecting your baby's natural rhythms—when they're hungry, tired, or ready to play—helps them feel understood and supported.

So finding balance is not about perfect schedules or rigid rules but about flexibility and connection. Responding to your baby's cues with patience and care teaches them that their needs matter and that they are safe to express themselves. Over time, this secure relationship helps your baby develop confidence and resilience.

Remember, you don't need to have all the answers. Follow your instincts, observe your baby's unique preferences, and be open to adjusting your approach as they grow.

Balance in the first year comes from honoring both your baby's individuality and your own parenting journey.

Reflective Questions

The first year of your baby's life is filled with profound changes, joyful moments, and inevitable challenges. As you reflect on this chapter, take time to think about your experiences, beliefs, and daily routines. The questions below are designed to help you explore your instincts, deepen your connection with your baby, and apply gentle parenting and Montessori principles in practical, meaningful ways. Use them as a guide to pause, reassess, and create a more intentional and responsive approach to your baby's first year.

1. Think about your expectations for your baby's first year— how do they compare to what you've learned about typical developmental milestones?

2. What insights from this Chapter can help you better respond to your baby's developmental needs in a supportive, gentle way?

3. How do you define success in your baby's development, and where might you need to shift your expectations to be more in line with gentle parenting principles?

4. How do you define success in your baby's development, and where might you need to shift your expectations to be more in line with gentle parenting principles?

5. How does viewing your baby as a capable communicator change your perspective on early interactions?

6. What elements of your home environment support your baby's ability to explore independently, and where could you make improvements?

7. How do your current strategies for sleep reflect your beliefs about comfort, independence, and routine?

8. What assumptions do you have about feeding practices, and how might they align or conflict with gentle parenting?

9. What are the most common sources of exhaustion or stress in your day-to-day life as a parent, and how could small changes help ease them?

10. How do you currently handle feeding struggles, and what new approaches might better support both you and your baby?

11. How does sleep deprivation affect your ability to parent with empathy and patience?

12. Reflect on your relationship with your partner—how has parenting together strengthened or challenged your bond?

Chapter Three

Little Steps, Big Changes -The Transition to Two

"If we change our whole attitude and say to ourselves, "My child knows what is best for him. Let us of course watch that he comes to no harm, but instead of trying to teach him our ways let us give him the freedom to live his little life in his own way," then perhaps, if we are observant, we shall learn something about the ways of childhood." —Maria Montessori.

Between 12 and 24 months, your toddler's development will leave you in awe. It's an exciting time, filled with growth and change, and you'll be thrilled and challenged by their rapid progress. One moment, they're just beginning to toddle, and the next, they're running, climbing, and navigating the world with a newfound confidence. The physical transformation can feel like a whirlwind—your child's hands become more dexterous, their coordination improves, and their energy seems boundless.

As your child's physical abilities grow, so does their desire for independence. Phrases like "Me do it!" and "Mine!" become more frequent as they assert control over their world. While this is a crucial part of their development, at times it can be challenging to manage.

The balance between honoring their growing autonomy and ensuring their safety can feel like a constant push and pull. You might find yourself wrestling with the desire to step in and help, versus stepping back to allow them the space to explore and learn. Recognizing their developmental drive for independence will help you approach these moments patiently, knowing that it's a natural part of their growth.

In addition to their physical and emotional evolution, your toddler's language skills will take off. At times, you may feel like a translator, as they try to express themselves with new words—and sometimes frustration when they can't quite get their point across. This period is full of trial and error, both for your child and for you.

You'll begin to notice them experimenting with two-word combinations and slowly forming short sentences. Your responses to their words—whether through encouragement, validation, or helping them expand their vocabulary—will create a foundation for their future communication skills.

While this stage is exhilarating, it's also emotionally demanding. You'll be managing a lot of "no" moments with your child who is learning to assert their will, and dealing with their constant attempts to assert their independence. It may feel overwhelming at times, but as you watch your child gain confidence and find their voice, the rewards will feel immeasurable.

So in this chapter, we'll look at toddlerhood through the lenses of play, boundaries, and emotional regulation. Let's start with the fun stuff - playtime!

Add Montessori Magic to Playing, Learning, and Thriving

The Montessori philosophy shines brightly in the toddler years, offering a framework to encourage self-directed exploration and learning. At this stage, children are driven by a strong sense of curiosity and an emerging desire for independence. So creating a prepared environment that supports these developmental needs can empower your child, building confidence and a love of learning from an early age.

Setting Up a Prepared Environment

Montessori environments are designed to be child-centric, meaning everything is accessible and organized in a way that invites toddlers to engage. Think of your home as a place where your toddler is free to explore safely, with spaces set up to support their developmental milestones.

Furniture should be child-sized, from low tables and chairs to shelves where toys and activities are within easy reach. Instead of overflowing toy bins, Montessori-inspired spaces feature a few thoughtfully selected activities arranged neatly. This helps your little one focus on one thing at a time and fosters a sense of order.

When choosing toys and materials, aim for those that encourage open-ended play and problem-solving. Wooden blocks, nesting cups, simple puzzles, and activities that involve stacking or sorting are excellent options. Toddlers learn through hands-on experience, so items that engage their senses are especially beneficial.

Maria Montessori once said, *"The hands are the instruments of man's intelligence."* By offering materials they can manipulate, you're giving your toddler the opportunity to develop fine motor skills and explore cause and effect at their own pace.

Hands-On Fun for Growing Skills

Here are some suggestions to spark your ideas for playtime fun.

Simple Sensory Bins (Rice, Oats, or Pasta)

Sensory bins are a fantastic way to engage your toddler's senses and fine motor skills. The act of scooping, pouring, and sifting helps develop hand-eye coordination and strengthens their fingers, preparing them for future tasks like writing. Using natural materials, such as rice, oats, or pasta, aligns with Montessori's emphasis on real-world experiences.

How to Set It Up.

- Fill a shallow container with your chosen material (uncooked rice, oats, or pasta).

- Add scoops, small cups, and spoons for exploration.

- Consider including small natural objects, such as pinecones or smooth pebbles, for added texture and variety.

- Introduce themed sensory bins, like adding toy animals to create a "farm," or dyed pasta in seasonal colors for creative play.

Safety Tip. Always supervise closely to prevent accidental ingestion or choking. For younger toddlers, larger pasta shapes (e.g., penne or rigatoni) are a safer option.

Finger Painting with Edible Paints

Finger painting gives toddlers the freedom to express themselves creatively while exploring textures and colors. Using edible paints ensures safety, as toddlers often put their fingers in their mouths. The activity promotes sensory integration, hand-eye coordination, and motor skill development while encouraging a sense of wonder as they mix colors and create patterns.

How to Set It Up.

- Make edible paint using yogurt mixed with natural food coloring or pureed fruits and vegetables.

- Provide sturdy paper or a wipeable surface for painting.

- Encourage your toddler to explore freely with their hands, but you can also suggest simple shapes like handprints or dots.

- Talk about the colors and textures they're experiencing to enhance language development.

Safety Tip. Use non-toxic, food-safe ingredients, and protect your surfaces with a washable mat or old newspapers.

Playdough Exploration

Playdough offers endless opportunities for tactile exploration, creativity, and fine motor skill development. Squishing, rolling, and molding help strengthen small hand muscles, which are critical for later tasks like writing and using utensils. Homemade, natural playdough adds a sensory component while ensuring it's safe for little ones.

How to Set It Up.

- Make your own playdough using simple ingredients like flour, salt, water, and natural food coloring. Add scents like vanilla or cinnamon for extra sensory appeal.

- Provide cookie cutters, small rolling pins, or blunt utensils for shaping and cutting.

- Introduce nature-inspired play by adding dried flowers, leaves, or herbs to the dough.

Safety Tip. Supervise closely to ensure toddlers don't eat too much of the dough, even if it's made with safe ingredients.

Outdoor Nature Collection

Exploring and collecting natural items like leaves, rocks, or flowers helps toddlers connect with the environment, promotes respect for nature, and introduces early categorization skills. It's a wonderful opportunity to develop observational skills and practice sorting by size, color, or texture.

How to Set It Up.

- Head to a nearby park, garden, or even your backyard.

- Give your toddler a small basket or container to collect items like leaves, pinecones, or smooth stones.

- Back at home, set up a sorting activity where they group items by color, shape, or texture.

- Extend the activity by creating simple crafts, such as leaf rubbings or painting rocks.

Safety Tip. Be mindful of sharp or toxic plants and ensure your child doesn't put small items in their mouth. Choose outdoor spaces that are safe and toddler-friendly.

Water Play with Pouring and Scooping

Water play introduces concepts including volume and cause-and-effect while enhancing motor skills. It also offers a calming sensory experience.

How to Set It Up.

- Fill a shallow basin or large bowl with water.

- Add small pitchers, cups, and spoons for pouring and scooping.

- Include floating objects like rubber ducks or natural materials like corks and leaves.

- Introduce food coloring or safe bath paints for added excitement.

Safety Tip. Always supervise water play to ensure safety, even with shallow water.

Stacking and Nesting Toys

Why. These toys develop spatial awareness, hand-eye coordination, and problem-solving skills while introducing early math concepts like size and order.

How to Set It Up.

- Provide wooden stacking rings, nesting cups, or blocks.

- Encourage your child to explore stacking by size or shape, or let them knock structures down for fun.

- For a natural twist, use smooth stones or wooden discs.

Safety Tip. Ensure all pieces are non-toxic, free of small parts, and sturdy.

Indoor Sensory Walk

An indoor sensory walk engages multiple senses and encourages movement and exploration. It also helps toddlers connect with their environment.

How to Set It Up.

- Create a simple sensory pathway using items such as soft rugs, bubble wrap, smooth wood, and grass mats.

- Let your toddler walk barefoot over each surface and describe how it feels.

- Take the concept outdoors by walking on sand, pebbles, or grass.

Safety Tip. Inspect all materials for safety and keep sharp or hazardous items out of reach.

Large Cardboard Box Play

A large cardboard box fosters creativity and imaginative play, allowing toddlers to explore spatial awareness and problem-solving.

How to Set It Up.

- Provide a large, clean cardboard box.

- Cut out windows or doors to turn it into a "house" or "car."

- Offer crayons for decorating or use the box as a tunnel to crawl through.

Safety Tip. Remove staples or sharp edges from the box and supervise play to prevent tipping.

Kitchen Helper Activities

Including toddlers in simple kitchen tasks promotes practical life skills, independence, and motor development.

How to Set It Up.

- Have them "help" with tasks like washing fruit, stirring batter, or scooping flour with measuring cups.

- Use a child-safe stool or a learning tower for safety and accessibility.

- Encourage them to explore kitchen tools like silicone spatulas or measuring spoons.

Safety Tip. Keep hot or sharp items out of reach and supervise closely.

Bubble Fun

Chasing and popping bubbles develops gross motor skills, coordination, and focus.

How to Set It Up.

- Use a bubble wand or machine to create bubbles.

- Encourage your toddler to catch them or stomp them when they land on the ground.

- Introduce simple counting, such as "How many bubbles can you pop?"

Safety Tip. Use a non-toxic bubble solution and play in a safe, open area.

Simple Hide-and-Seek with Objects

This activity promotes memory, focus, and problem-solving.

How to Set It Up.

- Hide a favorite toy under a blanket or inside a box and encourage your toddler to find it.

- Gradually make the game more challenging by hiding objects in different parts of the room.

- Narrate what's happening to build language skills, e.g., "Where is the ball? Is it under the chair?"

Safety Tip. Avoid small objects that could be a choking hazard during the game.

Bringing It All Together

These activities not only entertain but also nurture your toddler's curiosity and skills. By combining open-ended exploration with safe, natural materials, you're fostering creativity, independence, and a love for learning—all while creating precious moments of connection.

Encourage your child to take the lead and adapt each activity to their unique interests and their developmental stage.

Encouraging Practical Life Skills

A hallmark of the Montessori approach is the emphasis on practical life activities. Toddlers are capable of participating in everyday tasks, and involving them in these routines encourages independence and a sense of belonging. Simple activities like pouring water from a small jug, wiping up spills, putting away toys, or helping to wash vegetables for dinner can make them feel capable and involved.

Naturally, these tasks may take longer or be messier than if you did them yourself, but they offer incredible learning opportunities. For example, letting your toddler help with meal preparation builds coordination and patience. They also learn sequencing. understanding that an apple needs to be cut before it can be eaten, for instance. Helping to unpack the dishwasher by handing spoons to a parent for sorting or setting up their place at the table are other simple ways to involve them.

If you have a garden, provide child-sized spades and rakes and encourage your toddler to participate in outdoor chores like planting seeds or helping to water plants. Making them a part of family duties as soon as possible helps them see themselves as valued contributors. You will be surprised by how these activities increase confidence as your child feels capable and contributes to the family unit in practical ways.

When introducing these activities, start small and be patient. Demonstrate each step slowly and clearly, using simple language. Toddlers thrive on repetition, so give them plenty of chances to practice, and avoid stepping in to correct unless they're frustrated or unsafe. This approach not only builds motor skills but also reinforces the idea that mistakes are a natural part of learning.

Growing Strong through Outdoor Fun

Montessori philosophy doesn't end indoors. Outdoor play is vital for toddlers to develop their gross motor skills and experience the natural world. Consider setting up opportunities for movement and exploration outside.

Simple activities like digging in the dirt, climbing small structures, or collecting leaves are rich with learning opportunities. Encourage your child to engage all their senses. feeling the texture of bark, listening to birds, or splashing in puddles. These experiences are not only joyful but also help them develop balance, coordination, and an appreciation for nature.

Whether indoors or outside, the goal is to support your toddler's development in a way that feels natural and joyful. The Montessori approach is about respecting your child's innate drive to learn and grow, giving them space to become active participants in their world.

As you incorporate these ideas into daily life and combine them with your gentle parenting approach, you create an environment where self-directed learning and exploration are celebrated, laying the foundation for a confident and capable child.

Outings to Spark Curiosity and Growth

Toddlers thrive on exploration, and short, enriching outings can offer new experiences that stimulate their senses, promote development, and deepen their connection to the world around them. While these excursions can be incredibly rewarding, they require careful planning to ensure your little one remains safe, engaged, and happy. Toddlers love to explore but can also wander off in excitement, so always keep a close eye and use tools like harnesses, strollers, or child-friendly backpacks when needed.

Here are some ideas for outings that can create joyful learning opportunities while keeping your child's safety in mind.

Petting Zoo or Farm Visit

Toddlers are naturally curious about animals, and a petting zoo or farm visit provides a rich, multisensory experience. They can touch soft fur, hear the clucks and bleats of animals, and see them up close. These experiences help build empathy and emotional connection as your child learns to be gentle with animals.

Use the visit to expand their language skills by naming animals and mimicking their sounds. Encourage them to describe what they see, hear, and feel, fostering observation and descriptive language.

Safety Tip. Ensure the environment is child-friendly, with barriers to keep animals and toddlers safe. Supervise closely to prevent accidental roughness with animals.

Library Storytime

Libraries often host free storytime sessions tailored to young children. These outings expose toddlers to books, songs, and rhymes, building early literacy and comprehension skills. They also encourage social interaction as your child observes and engages with other children.

Choose a session with an age-appropriate theme, and follow up by borrowing books on similar topics to extend the experience at home. Toddlers will enjoy repeating songs and phrases they heard during storytime.

Safety Tip. Keep your child within arm's reach as libraries often have open spaces, and little ones may wander in their excitement.

Music and Movement Class

Toddlers naturally respond to music and rhythm, and a structured class can enhance their motor skills, coordination, and social awareness. Participating in simple dances or playing child-sized instruments also introduces pattern recognition and fosters creativity.

Look for classes that include interactive songs and activities, encouraging your child to explore rhythm and sound through movement and play. Join in to model participation and make the experience more engaging.

Safety Tip. Watch out for slippery floors or crowded spaces, ensuring your toddler has plenty of room to move safely.

Nature Walks in a Local Park

Spending time outdoors fosters a love for nature, strengthens gross motor skills, and provides opportunities to explore textures, colors, and sounds. Picking up leaves, observing insects, or splashing in puddles makes the experience exciting and memorable.

Turn the outing into a mini scavenger hunt by encouraging your toddler to find specific items, like a yellow leaf or a smooth rock. Let them set the pace, stopping to explore whatever catches their interest.

Safety Tip. Keep to safe, toddler-friendly paths and stay alert near water or uneven terrain. A lightweight harness or child leash can offer extra peace of mind.

Visit to a Children's Museum or Science Center

Many children's museums have exhibits designed specifically for toddlers, featuring hands-on activities that spark curiosity and encourage problem-solving. These settings allow toddlers to explore at their own pace in a controlled environment.

Look for exhibits with sensory play areas, simple cause-and-effect activities, or opportunities to build and create. Engage your child by asking open-ended questions like, "What happens if we do this?"

Safety Tip. Many museums have designated toddler zones, which are safer for younger children. Stay nearby as toddlers can easily become distracted and wander.

Splash Pads or Shallow Pools

Water play is an exciting sensory experience for toddlers, promoting physical development as they run, splash, and experiment with cause and effect.

Bring toys like buckets or watering cans to encourage imaginative play. Use the opportunity to introduce concepts like filling and pouring.

Safety Tip. Never leave your child unattended around water, even in shallow areas, and ensure they have non-slip footwear.

Farmer's Market Stroll

A trip to the market exposes your toddler to vibrant sights, smells, and tastes. Sampling fresh produce and seeing where food comes from builds curiosity about nutrition and the world around them.

Involve your child by letting them pick out a fruit or vegetable, and talk about colors, textures, and tastes. This can be a great way to encourage picky eaters to try something new.

Safety Tip. Crowds can be overwhelming for toddlers, so stay close and use a stroller or carrier if needed.

Simple Errands with a Twist

Even everyday outings, like going to the grocery store, can become exciting adventures for toddlers. These trips introduce new environments and provide opportunities for practical learning.

Turn errands into interactive experiences by involving your toddler. Let them help pick out items or count objects. Praise their contributions to build their confidence.

Safety Tip. Keep the outing short and bring snacks or small toys to manage boredom.

Bringing It All Together

These excursions not only enrich your child's development but also create special moments of connection. Whether it's the joy of petting a goat, the thrill of jumping in a puddle, or the quiet focus during storytime, your toddler is learning about themselves and the world. By combining gentle parenting and Montessori principles—respecting their need for exploration while providing structure and safety—you're fostering a love of learning that will last a lifetime.

Encouraging Language Development

> 'The way we talk to our children becomes their inner voice' —Peggy O'Mara.

Language acquisition is a core aspect of this developmental stage, and gentle parenting and Montessori approaches both advocate for rich, meaningful communication.

Use everyday moments as teaching opportunities. Montessori educators often talk about the "absorbent mind," where young children absorb language from their surroundings effortlessly. Speak to your child with clarity, narrating your actions to build vocabulary. For example, as you prepare lunch, explain, "I'm cutting this apple. It's crunchy and juicy." These real-life experiences enrich their understanding of words and concepts.

Pause and Listen

As your toddler begins to express themselves, giving them time to find their words will help them. Resist the urge to finish their sentences or rush their speech. Instead, get down to their level, make eye contact, and show that you value what they have to say. This practice not only fosters language skills but also reinforces their sense of self-worth.

Fostering Independent Play

Both approaches underscore the importance of self-directed play as a way for toddlers to build confidence, problem-solving abilities, and focus. Montessori emphasizes creating a prepared environment that encourages autonomy and exploration.

Design a Child-Centric Space

Arrange your home in a way that empowers your toddler to engage in independent play. Use low shelves for toys and activities, and provide child-sized furniture to foster a sense of ownership. Montessori-inspired play areas are clutter-free, with a limited selection of open-ended materials like blocks, nesting cups, or simple puzzles. Rotating toys every few weeks keeps the environment stimulating and encourages deeper engagement.

Trust Your Toddler's Ability to Play Independently

It can be tempting to jump in and direct your child's play, but giving them the freedom to explore builds problem-solving skills and resilience. Stand back and observe, offering help only if truly necessary.

For example, if your toddler struggles to fit a puzzle piece, you might say, "You're working hard on that puzzle. Let me know if you need some help," instead of stepping in right away. This approach reflects the values of gentle parenting and Montessori, reinforcing your trust in their abilities.

Model and Encourage Purposeful Work

Montessori emphasizes the idea of "work" even for the youngest children. Toddlers love to imitate adults, so involve them in simple, age-appropriate household tasks.

This could mean letting them help wash vegetables, wipe down tables, or water plants. These activities are confidence-boosting experiences that promote independence and a sense of contribution to the family. As you invite your toddler to participate, use encouraging language, and show appreciation for their efforts, no matter how imperfect.

By integrating these practical strategies, you create a balance that nurtures your toddler's independence while respecting their developmental needs. This blended approach empowers your child to explore and learn at their own pace, all within the safety of a loving and respectful relationship. Trust in your ability to observe and adapt, and remember that the connection you build now lays the foundation for a confident, self-assured child.

Nurturing Discipline and Autonomy.

Building Words, Play Skills, and Boundaries

As your toddler develops, the key to nurturing their independence while setting appropriate boundaries lies in blending the empathetic gentle parenting ethos with Montessori-inspired principles of independence and discovery. Both approaches emphasize respect for the child as an individual and the importance of fostering a strong emotional connection while creating an environment where they can learn through exploration and practice.

Balancing Boundaries with Empathy

Every toddler parent will confirm that setting boundaries is essential. Gentle parenting teaches us to do this in a way that respects the toddler's growing sense of autonomy. In a Montessori context, boundaries are viewed as tools to guide rather than control. When your toddler pushes limits—which they inevitably will—it's an opportunity to practice consistency paired with compassion.

Frame Limits in a Positive Way

Instead of focusing on what the child shouldn't do, emphasize what they can do. For example, rather than saying, "Don't run inside," try, "We walk when we're indoors to stay safe." This subtle shift aligns with gentle parenting and Montessori philosophies, encouraging cooperation and helping your child understand the 'why' behind a rule.

Involve Your Child in Problem-Solving

Montessori principles suggest that children are more likely to respect boundaries if they feel part of the decision-making process. When conflicts arise, involve your toddler in finding a solution. If they're upset about leaving the playground, you might say, "We need to go home now, but what should we do when we get there? Would you like to help make a snack or read a book?" This gives your child a sense of agency and reinforces the idea that their opinions matter.

Staying Steady Through Emotional Storms

Toddlers test, and that's exactly what they are supposed to do. A toddler has failed if he makes life too easy for us." —Janet Lansbury.

Toddlerhood is a time of tremendous emotional growth, and big feelings often come with the territory. Meltdowns and tantrums are not only normal but also a sign that your child is learning to navigate their emotions. Understanding this can help you approach these outbursts with patience and empathy, staying true to your gentle parenting principles even under pressure.

Keep Your Cool When Emotions Run High

At those moments when your toddler is overwhelmed, staying calm can feel incredibly challenging, especially when outside judgment or unwanted advice is added to the mix.

Sticking to your principles means acknowledging that your child's emotional outbursts are part of their developmental journey, not something to be "fixed" for the comfort of others.

It's not always going to be easy, but maintaining your composure is key to modeling the kind of emotional regulation you want your child to learn. Remember. your child is not giving you a hard time; they are having a hard time. Take a moment to breathe deeply, ground yourself, and remind yourself that your calm presence is exactly what they need.

"Meltdowns and tantrums can be valuable moments for parents to strengthen their bond with their child. Approach them with compassion, patience, and a willingness to understand." —Dr. Ross Greene.

If a single deep breath isn't enough, and you feel yourself reacting emotionally as frustration rises, try counting to five in your head or even stepping away briefly (ensuring your child is safe) to collect your thoughts. This pause can prevent knee-jerk reactions and help you respond from a place of calm rather than stress. These responses are not about suppressing your own feelings but about being mindful of how they impact your interactions with your child.

But sticking to your principles means acknowledging that your child's emotional outbursts are part of their developmental journey, not something to be "fixed" for the comfort of others.

> You haven't known suffering until you've taken a 2-year-old shopping for a birthday gift that isn't for them." —OutnumberedMother (@OutNumbMother)

Example. Staying Consistent in Public

Imagine you're at the grocery store, and your toddler has a meltdown because they want a treat. You feel the heat of judgmental eyes, and the temptation to pacify your child in any way you can be strong.

In moments like these, remember the long-term goal. teaching your child how to manage disappointment. Instead of giving in, get down to their level, acknowledge their feelings with empathy—"You really wanted that treat, and it's so hard when we can't have what we want"—and hold firm to your boundary.

Yes, it's uncomfortable, but you're demonstrating to your child that emotions are acceptable, and boundaries are loving.

Navigating Unwanted Advice

Lastly, when faced with those judgments or unwanted parenting advice, remember that your choices reflect your values, not anyone else's. It's okay to thank someone for their concern and not engage further. Phrases like "Thanks, we're handling it in our own way" or simply changing the subject can be a kind but firm way to maintain your boundaries.

Above all, be gentle with yourself. You're not expected to have all the answers or remain serene at all times. What matters is that you keep trying, keep learning, and keep showing up with love and patience for your child—and for yourself. By staying grounded in your principles and giving yourself grace, you model the very qualities you hope to instill in your child.

Gentle Parenting Starts with Being Gentle on Yourself

> "As the months and years went by, I learned that the best way to help my son (and his three siblings who followed) to sleep and to regulate his emotions, was through connection, meeting his needs and helping him to feel safe and secure. I began to learn his triggers and how to avoid them, and how to de-escalate him when his big feelings threatened to boil over. We were both so much happier. Slowly, I learned to trust my instincts to nurture my son and to place his needs above the opinions of others."
> —Sara Ockwell-Smith

Setting boundaries with empathy starts with showing that same empathy to yourself. It's easy to feel inadequate or question your approach, especially when all those self-proclaimed "parenting experts" around you look disapprovingly and judge you harshly for being 'too soft'. But no one knows your child as well as you do, and trusting your instincts is crucial. Remind yourself that you're doing the best you can in each moment, and it's okay if not every response is perfect.

Self-Compassion Strategies

Debrief After Difficult Moments

After a particularly tough episode, give yourself the space to reflect on what happened without judgment. What worked well? What could you try differently next time? Remember, this isn't about criticizing yourself but about learning and growing alongside your child.

Seek Support Without Judgment

If you need to talk about your challenges, choose your support system wisely. Surround yourself with people who respect your parenting choices and can offer encouragement rather than unsolicited advice. Online communities focused on gentle parenting can also be a great resource for connecting with like-minded parents.

Celebrate Small Wins

Progress in toddlerhood often comes in tiny steps. Maybe your child waited two extra seconds before getting frustrated, or perhaps they tried using words to express a feeling. Celebrate these small victories, knowing that your gentle, consistent approach is laying the groundwork for emotional resilience.

Final Thoughts - Embracing the Joys and Demands of Early Toddlerhood

The toddler years bring a whirlwind of discovery, laughter, and new challenges. As your child begins to walk, explore, and assert their independence, you may find yourself constantly navigating the delicate balance of providing freedom within limits. This stage can be exhausting, but it's also a beautiful time to witness the wonder and curiosity with which your child approaches the world.

Each moment—whether it's a first word, a spontaneous hug, or the way they light up when mastering a new skill—reflects the foundation you're building. You're not just guiding them through milestones;

you're teaching them how to approach life with confidence, kindness, and resilience.

Both **gentle parenting** and **Montessori principles** offer valuable insights to support you during this transformative time. Gentle parenting emphasizes meeting your child's emotional needs with empathy and consistency, recognizing their struggles as they grapple with big feelings they're not yet equipped to manage. Montessori principles encourage you to nurture your child's independence, with opportunities to engage in purposeful activities and make choices within a structured environment. Together, these approaches create a harmonious framework that supports your child's growth.

For instance, when your toddler insists on doing something "all by myself," gentle parenting invites you to validate their need for autonomy while offering calm guidance through frustration. Meanwhile, the Montessori approach empowers you to prepare an environment that makes independence achievable—whether that's providing a low shelf with accessible toys or allowing them to pour their own water from a child-sized pitcher.

These early years are overflowing with moments of deep connection. Your toddler's spontaneous hug, their triumphant smile after mastering a new skill, or the way they light up when you join them in their play are reflections of the secure foundation you're building together. Gentle parenting helps strengthen this bond by encouraging respectful communication and nurturing trust. Montessori principles complement this by developing confidence and showing your child that their efforts are valued.

Yes, there will be tantrums and big emotions, days that test your patience, and times when you question if you're doing it "right." But each time you approach your child with empathy and stay true to your values, you're planting seeds of trust and emotional strength that will serve them for a lifetime.

By weaving the principles of gentle parenting and Montessori together, you're providing your child with the tools to explore the world with curiosity and joy while feeling secure in their place within it. The bond you're building now will not only support them through toddlerhood but also serve as a source of connection and strength for years to come.

So take a deep breath, celebrate the little wins, and remember— you've got this. Your dedication, patience, and love are exactly what your child needs. You're only helping them grow; you're growing alongside them. As you move through these joyful and challenging early years, trust that the bond you're creating now will be a source of connection, support, and pride for years to come.

Reflective Questions

Toddlerhood brings a mix of wonder, independence, and intense emotions. This period of rapid growth requires patience, flexibility, and a strong foundation of respectful parenting. The following questions invite you to reflect deeply on your experiences, explore the impact of your own upbringing on your parenting choices, and consider practical ways to integrate gentle parenting and Montessori principles. Use these reflections to approach this unique stage with confidence, empathy, and intentionality.

1. In what ways do your own experiences with independence as a child influence your current parenting choices?

2. Reflect on a recent moment of progress—what did it teach you about your toddler's unique way of learning?

3. How do your own childhood experiences with discipline influence your current beliefs about boundaries and punishment?

4. How do you feel when your toddler tests limits, and how might reframing those moments as opportunities for learning affect your response?

5. How do you decide when to offer guidance versus allowing your toddler to struggle or problem-solve on their own?

6. What practical opportunities can you create for your toddler to participate in everyday tasks?

7. What current discipline strategies are working well, and which feel ineffective or misaligned with gentle parenting?

8. How do you react when your toddler resists or refuses a request, and how could empathy play a stronger role in those moments?

9. How does understanding the root cause of tantrums change your perspective on them?

10. Reflect on a recent challenging moment—how did you handle it, and what would you like to try differently next time?

Chapter Four

Thriving in the Dynamic World of the Terrific Twos

As your little one transitions from early toddlerhood into the "Terrible Twos," you may find yourself on an emotional rollercoaster. This stage marks a time of intense change—not just for your child, who is navigating major leaps in their emotional, social, and cognitive development, but also for you as you learn to adapt to a new rhythm of independence and boundary-testing.

Between the ages of two and three, your child's sense of self blossoms. They're discovering who they are, where their limits lie, and how their actions affect others. This can sometimes feel like being caught in a whirlwind of surprising behavior, unexpected defiance, and big, occasionally overwhelming emotions. Moments of resistance, dramatic meltdowns, and relentless curiosity can leave you exhausted as your patience is tested in ways you could never have imagined.

One of the most common challenges parents face is achieving a balance between nurturing this newfound independence and setting the limits that keep life manageable for everyone. Your child is not just testing boundaries to challenge you but to gain an understanding of their place in the world. Yet the tug-of-war between granting freedom and maintaining structure can feel never-ending, requiring reserves of patience you never thought you'd need.

In this chapter, we'll explore ways to embrace your child's growing autonomy while you also guide them with gentleness and consistency. We'll discuss strategies to help you stay calm in the face of chaos, tools to nurture their social and emotional skills, and ways to celebrate the small victories that come with each new challenge.

While the "Terrible Twos" may be tough at times, they're also an incredible window into your child's blossoming creativity, empathy, and resilience, with milestones that will fill you with joy and pride.

Ultimately, this stage isn't just about your child's growth; it's also about your own. It's an opportunity to find grace in imperfection and discover new depths of patience. Every moment that tests you is also a chance to connect, guide, and cherish the journey you're on together. So, take a deep breath—you've got this.

From Me to We - Cultivating Empathetic Relationships

As your child moves further into toddlerhood, you'll likely notice a shift in how they engage with the world around them. Suddenly, social and emotional skills become a major focus, and so does your role in nurturing these new ways of connecting. At this age, toddlers are often eager to interact with their peers, navigating the complexities of sharing space, toys, and your attention. But as exciting as this stage can be, it also introduces unique challenges that may, just sometimes, test your patience and creativity.

Watching your little one as they begin to understand that others have feelings—even if they can't yet fully express their own—can be both heartwarming and frustrating. For the first time, they're learning what it means to be part of a community, and those early interactions are full of growth opportunities. But they're also rich with emotional ups and downs, requiring you to guide your little one through the process of building friendships and handling conflict.

One of the most beautiful, yet unpredictable, developments at this stage is the emergence of empathy. Around the age of two, your child may start to grasp that others have feelings, showing concern for friends or family members. Maybe they'll offer a toy to comfort a crying friend or gently pat someone who seems sad.

These small but meaningful moments are a testament to their growing sense of compassion, and they also offer you a chance to model and reinforce empathetic behavior. Describing emotions, narrating how actions affect others, and gently guiding your child in acts of kindness can make a big impact.

Of course, these breakthroughs don't come without setbacks. It's completely normal for toddlers to struggle with sharing, experience emotional outbursts, or have trouble negotiating over who gets the coveted red truck. As they encounter new situations, they learn problem-solving skills that sometimes feel messy and chaotic. You might see your child maneuvering around play obstacles, working to reach a toy, or arguing over turns on the slide. In these moments, your job is to provide the kind of support that fosters resilience.

Montessori principles, which encourage children to find solutions independently with minimal intervention, can be particularly helpful in teaching patience and perseverance.

This journey often demands deep reserves of calm and flexibility. You're managing moments of frustration as your little one learns to balance their desires with the needs of others.

Teaching empathy and sharing can feel exhausting, especially when your child's emotions seem larger than life and your patience is running thin. Yet every challenge is also a chance for growth—yours and theirs.

To help navigate these tricky moments, here are some strategies that can help to relieve the pressure.

- **Practice Deep Breathing and Self-Regulation.** When emotions run high, take a few deep breaths to calm yourself before responding to your child. Modeling calm behavior not only helps you but also shows your toddler how to self-regulate in challenging situations.

- **Set Realistic Expectations.** Remember that your child is still learning and developing. It's entirely normal for them to struggle with sharing or managing big feelings. Also, set realistic expectations for yourself—parenting is a journey, and you're allowed to have hard days as you learn and grow alongside your child.

- **Take Breaks When Needed.** If a situation becomes overwhelming, permit yourself to step away briefly if it's safe. A short pause can help you reset and respond with more patience and clarity.

- **Connect with a Support Network.** Parenting through the toddler years can feel isolating, but it doesn't have to be. Talking to other parents, joining a parenting group, or simply reaching out to friends can provide reassurance and fresh perspectives.

- **Celebrate Small Victories.** Acknowledge your child's progress, even if it seems minor. Recognizing positive moments can uplift your spirits and reinforce the behaviors you want to encourage.

Amid toddlerhood's unpredictable moments, remember that you're building a foundation of empathy, resilience, and love. Each triumph and every setback offers an opportunity to deepen your shared bond, creating a journey filled with growth, connection, and endless possibilities.

Navigating 'No!'. Turning Defiance into Connection

> *"So can you tell us what makes you qualified for the position of hostage negotiator?"*
>
> *"I have a 2 year old."*
>
> *"You're hired."*
>
> — *full metal mommy (@FullMetalMommy), 2015*

Encourage Independence and Creativity

A Montessori-inspired approach to supporting your toddler's growing independence includes letting them make choices and experiment in a safe and guided way.

- **Offer Limited Choices.** Simple decisions, like choosing between two snacks or two different activities, help your toddler feel empowered and teach them how to make thoughtful choices. This practice also helps reduce power struggles, giving you both a greater sense of ease.

- **Allow for Safe Experimentation.** Encourage your toddler to try things on their own, whether it's climbing up a small step or stacking blocks. When you refrain from stepping in too quickly, your child learns through experience, and you have the chance to model patience and support.

- **Take a Step Back and Observe.** Sometimes, the best support you can offer is to step back and watch your toddler explore at their own pace. It's a chance for both of you to appreciate their growing abilities.

- **Trust Their Skills.** Maria Montessori advised, *"Never help a child with a task at which he feels he can succeed."* Giving your toddler time to figure out challenges on their own helps them build resilience, while also encouraging you to trust their capabilities—and your own as a guiding parent.

- **Observe and Connect.** Notice which activities captivate your child, whether it's stacking, sorting, or creative play. Understanding what interests them allows you to adjust their environment and support their natural curiosity, while also giving you a window into their world.

By making space for independence, you're helping your toddler become more confident, creative, and capable. And in doing so, you'll also find moments of connection and joy as you both discover new things about each other and the world around you.

Evolving Play for Growing Minds

As your toddler develops between 24–36 months, play activities and arts and crafts can evolve to reflect their growing fine motor skills, creativity, problem-solving abilities, and social awareness. Here are a few suggestions that build on activities from the earlier stage and align with Montessori principles.

Sorting and Categorizing

- Provide objects of varying colors, shapes, or sizes for your toddler to sort (e.g., buttons, blocks, or small toys).
- Progression. Introduce more complex categories, such as animals versus vehicles, or color and size combined.

Building and Stacking Challenges

- Offer blocks or interlocking building sets.
- Progression. Encourage constructing specific structures, like towers of certain heights or shapes like bridges.

Simple Puzzles

- Begin with puzzles featuring 4–8 pieces.

- Progression. Move to slightly more complex puzzles (10–12 pieces) with thematic pictures your child enjoys.

Pretend Play with Themes

- Create play scenarios with dolls, toy kitchens, or dress-up items.

- Progression. Introduce themes like "grocery shopping" with reusable bags, toy food, and even a pretend cash register to encourage role-playing and basic math.

Obstacle Courses

- Use pillows, cushions, or tunnels for climbing and crawling.

- Progression. Add balance beams, stepping stones, or simple challenges like hopping on one foot.

Baking Simple Recipes (Mixing Dough or Batter)

Involves multiple senses—touch, smell, taste—and introduces practical life skills. Promotes independence and coordination.

Sound Matching Game

Fill containers with different materials (beans, rice, bells) for children to shake and match by sound. Enhances auditory discrimination and memory.

All these activities nurture curiosity, build skills, and encourage exploration while fostering a calm, respectful environment—core to both gentle parenting and Montessori philosophies.

Arts and Craft-Themed Play

Sticker Collages

- Give your toddler colorful stickers to create pictures on blank paper.

- Progression. Encourage sorting stickers by theme (e.g., animals, shapes) and arranging them into patterns.

Painting with Tools

- Offer edible finger paints or brushes.

- Progression. Introduce sponges, rollers, or stamps for more intricate designs, focusing on layering colors or textures.

Cut-and-Paste Crafts

- Provide safety scissors and paper for cutting shapes, followed by gluing onto a larger sheet to create pictures.

- Progression. Use templates for them to cut along lines or craft specific shapes like trees or animals.

Playdough Sculpting

- Offer playdough and basic tools like cookie cutters or rolling pins.

- Progression. Encourage sculpting simple shapes or objects like balls, snakes, or basic figures.

Nature Art

- Collect leaves, sticks, or pebbles and create collages.

- Progression. Use natural items to create prints by pressing them into clay or painting and stamping them onto paper.

Stringing Beads

- Use large beads and a shoelace for threading.
- Progression. Move to smaller beads or pattern-making (e.g., alternating colors).

Watercolor Exploration

- Let your toddler experiment with watercolors.
- Progression. Show them how to blend colors or paint within simple shapes and outlines.

Montessori-Inspired Progressions

Practical Life Activities

- Washing vegetables, pouring water, or peeling a banana.
- Progression. Introduce simple meal prep like spreading butter with a blunt knife or using tongs to serve snacks.

Shape and Number Tracing

- Provide sandpaper numbers and shapes for tactile tracing.
- Progression. Transition to drawing shapes and numbers on paper.

Matching Games

- Start with matching identical cards or objects.

- Progression. Match related items, like a picture of an animal to a toy animal.

These activities provide natural progression for your toddler's growing abilities, encouraging independence, creativity, and motor skill development while keeping them fully engaged.

Real-World Explorations

Children's Science Museum

Why? Hands-on exhibits align with Montessori's experiential learning approach. Helps children explore cause-and-effect relationships and basic scientific concepts.

Community Garden or Farmers' Market

Why? Encourages an understanding of where food comes from, introduces new vocabulary, and promotes responsibility through small gardening tasks.

Historical Site or Local Cultural Festival

Why? Sparks curiosity about history and different cultures. Provides opportunities to discuss diversity and tradition, fostering respect and global awareness.

Animal Rescue Center or Aquarium

Why? Nurtures compassion and respect for living creatures. Observing different animals promotes observational skills and conversation.

These outings align with Montessori's emphasis on sensory learning, real-world exploration, and nurturing a child's innate curiosity. Each trip provides a developmentally appropriate opportunity to interact with the world, fostering cognitive, emotional, and social growth.

Navigating Screen Time with Confidence and Compassion

In today's digital age, screens are an undeniable part of life. Whether it's a tablet for a video call with grandparents or an educational app, technology is woven into our daily routines. Balancing screen time with other developmental needs can feel challenging. However, approaching this topic through the lens of gentle parenting and Montessori principles can transform screen time into an intentional aspect of your parenting journey. Here's how to find that balance.

Screen Time Without Guilt

First and foremost, release the guilt. Parenting in a world of technology means finding harmony rather than striving for perfection. Trust your instincts when it comes to what works best for your child and family. If screen time is part of your daily routine, it doesn't have to be a source of stress. The goal is mindful use that complements your child's exploration and growth.

Set Clear, Consistent Boundaries

Children between the ages of 2 and 3 thrive with structure, so establishing clear limits around screen time can create predictability and ease transitions. Decide on a routine that feels balanced, whether it's 20 minutes of screen time after lunch or an educational video before dinner. Clear boundaries help your child understand when screen time fits into their day and when it's time to engage in other activities. This consistency supports a gentle approach to discipline, where the focus is on guiding rather than restricting.

Choose Enriching, Interactive Content

The quality of screen time matters as much as the quantity. Opt for content that aligns with your values and supports learning through engagement. Look for shows or apps that are slow-paced and encourage participation, such as those that invite singing, dancing, or problem-solving.

Content that sparks curiosity or fosters storytelling can transform screen time into a moment of creative inspiration. By prioritizing enriching options, you can feel confident that screen time is serving as an additional tool in your child's learning journey.

Model Mindful Technology Use

Toddlers learn by watching you. If your phone is always in hand or you're absorbed by a screen during family time, they'll take note. Demonstrating responsible tech habits—such as putting your phone away during meals or playtime—reinforces that being present is a priority. This doesn't mean eliminating your screen use entirely, but showing balance helps them build their understanding of moderation.

Encourage Screen-Free Alternatives

Balance screen time by nurturing a love for activities that fuel independence and creativity. Montessori principles emphasize hands-on learning, so create spaces at home where your child can explore toys, art supplies, and sensory materials at their own pace. Rotating activities, such as a small puzzle area or a nature-inspired sensory bin, keep their curiosity engaged without turning to screens as a default.

Be Flexible and Trust Your Instincts

There will be days when screen time exceeds your usual limits, and that's okay. Trust that you know your child and what they need at that moment. If you're using screens to calm a tired toddler or connect during a busy day, remember that balance happens over time. Your instincts are your best guide, and gentle parenting emphasizes compassion for both your child and yourself.

Connect Screen Time to Real-Life Learning

Whenever possible, extend what your child sees on-screen to real-life exploration. If they watch a show about animals, take the opportunity to visit the park and look for birds or squirrels. This helps them make connections between the digital and physical world, fostering a deeper understanding and keeping their curiosity alive.

Approaching screen time with awareness and confidence can turn it from a source of worry to an integrated part of your gentle parenting approach. Remember, the way you navigate this aspect of life teaches your child about balance, mindfulness, and the value of both engagement and rest.

Building Bonds. Nurturing Social Skills and Play

As toddlers move from exploring the world individually to engaging with others, social skills such as empathy, sharing, and group dynamics begin to take root. These moments are full of opportunities to guide your child through new social experiences with patience and encouragement. Here's how to create a nurturing space for social growth and collaborative play.

Start with Small, Comfortable Playdates

Large groups can feel overwhelming to young toddlers who are just beginning to navigate social settings. Starting with one-on-one playdates or small family gatherings can create a safe, manageable space for your child to practice social interactions. Use these moments to observe how your child handles sharing, turn-taking, and personal space. Your role is to notice their cues and support them when needed, building their confidence for larger group experiences.

Guide Social Situations Rather than Intervene

Inevitably, toddlers will experience moments of frustration or conflict, such as squabbles over toys or boundaries. Before stepping in, give them a chance to solve problems on their own. This space helps them develop negotiation skills and learn resilience.

When needed, gently step in and model simple communication strategies, like, "You can say, 'Can I have a turn when you're done?'" This approach respects their independence while showing them constructive ways to engage with peers.

Encourage Moments of Empathy

Toddlers are just beginning to understand others' feelings, so fostering empathy is crucial at this stage. When another child is upset, prompt your toddler with phrases such as, "Oh, they look sad. Can we help?" These gentle nudges encourage them to recognize emotions in others and respond thoughtfully.

Over time, these small moments contribute to your child's ability to build strong, compassionate relationships.

Balance Collaborative and Independent Play

Play is the primary way toddlers learn about their world and develop social skills. Creating a balance between collaborative play and independent exploration can help your toddler grow in confidence and cooperation.

- **Provide Shared Activities.** Engage in simple, cooperative tasks like building a block tower together or working on a shared art project. These activities naturally teach patience, turn-taking, and teamwork while allowing you to model how to collaborate.

- **Encourage Self-Directed Play.** Time for unstructured play is equally important. Allowing your toddler to explore their toys and environment alone fosters resilience, independence, and problem-solving. While it may be tempting to join in, stepping back helps them learn to rely on their own ideas and creativity.

Celebrate Teamwork and Effort

When your child successfully engages in collaborative play—like building a fort or playing a simple game with friends—acknowledge their efforts in a way that emphasizes process over outcome. Try saying, "I noticed how you waited your turn and shared the blocks," to reinforce positive social behaviors. This type of feedback helps them see the value in cooperation and strengthens their desire to build positive connections.

By creating an environment that values empathy, patience, and collaborative play, you're helping your toddler develop essential social skills while nurturing their independence. This balance is a cornerstone of both gentle parenting and Montessori principles, guiding your child to grow with confidence and joy in their social interactions.

Potty Training. Patience, Positivity, and Progress

Potty training marks a significant step toward your toddler's independence and can test your patience and adaptability. This journey is often a mix of pride, uncertainty, and occasional frustration. Approaching it with an open mind, flexibility, and gentle encouragement can create a more positive experience for both of you.

Recognizing Your Child's Readiness

The pressure to start potty training can come from all directions—family, friends, or comparisons with peers. But potty training isn't a one-size-fits-all milestone; it's deeply personal and depends on your child's readiness. Signs like staying dry for longer periods, showing curiosity about bathroom habits, or expressing discomfort with soiled diapers can indicate that they're prepared to start.

Allow your child's cues to guide you. If these signs aren't there yet, waiting until they emerge can prevent frustration and make the process smoother. Trusting your intuition helps you stay aligned with your child's natural development and supports a more cooperative atmosphere.

Creating a Routine and Maintaining a Calm Environment

Potty training can seem overwhelming at first, but incorporating it into the daily routine makes it feel less daunting. Choose consistent times, such as after meals or before bedtime, to encourage sitting on the potty. The familiarity of a routine builds comfort and predictability, giving your toddler the space to adapt at their own pace.

Resistance is common, but keeping a calm demeanor can work wonders. Your child will take cues from your response—if you're relaxed and patient, they'll sense that trying is safe and stress-free. The message is simple: learning is a process, and every small step counts.

Celebrating Progress Without Pressure

Each little success—whether it's sitting on the potty or attempting without results—deserves recognition. These moments are building blocks for your child's confidence and motivation. Simple phrases like "Great job trying!" or a warm smile can encourage them without attaching their worth to outcomes.

The goal is to strike a balance between positive reinforcement and keeping the process lighthearted. By focusing on effort rather than results, you help them develop resilience and view challenges as opportunities, not setbacks.

Managing Setbacks with Compassion

Regressions and accidents are part of the process. It's easy to feel disheartened after a series of accidents, but how you respond to these moments really matters. Learning is rarely a straight path, and setbacks are to be expected.

When accidents happen, take a breath and remind yourself that this is temporary. Remaining composed and reassuring your child with phrases like, "That's okay, we'll try again next time," helps create a safe environment for them to continue learning. This kind of response teaches them that mistakes are not failures but opportunities to try again, with your support.

Listening to Your Voice Among External Opinions

It's almost inevitable that you'll come across advice - solicited or not - from friends, family, and online sources. While some tips can be helpful, remember that no one knows your child as well as you do. You understand their temperament, preferences, and pace better than any general guideline or outside voice determined to share their experiences with you.

Staying confident in your choices, even when they diverge from conventional wisdom, reinforces that you're in tune with your child's needs. Trust that your approach, based on your unique understanding of your little one, will guide you through the process.

Showing Yourself Compassion on the Journey

Potty training is a learning experience for both you and your child. Some days may leave you feeling accomplished, while others may test your patience. Embrace the learning curve and practice self-kindness when things don't go as planned. Your composure and adaptability serve as powerful examples of resilience for your child.

Each phase in this stage holds moments to celebrate, opportunities to strengthen your bond, and lessons that shape both of you. By approaching potty training with patience, trust, and flexibility, you build a positive experience that supports your child's growth and your confidence in your parenting journey.

Handling Setbacks. When Things Don't Go as Planned

Even the best-laid plans and parenting strategies can seem to fall apart at times. In these moments, it's crucial to extend grace—not just to your child, but also to yourself. Gentle parenting and Montessori principles remind us to focus on learning and connection over perfection. Setbacks are learning opportunities, for you as well as your child. Here are some common scenarios and strategies to navigate them with compassion and understanding.

Scenario 1. The Public Meltdown

Your toddler has a full-blown tantrum in the grocery store because they want a snack you didn't plan to buy. You feel the weight of judgmental stares from every direction and your frustration mounting.

What to Do?

- **Pause and Regulate Yourself.** Take a deep breath and remind yourself that your toddler's behavior is a normal developmental stage, not a reflection of your parenting.

- **Acknowledge Their Feelings.** Kneel to their level and calmly say, "I see that you're upset because you wanted the snack. It's hard when we can't have what we want."

- **Redirect or Offer a Choice.** If possible, redirect them with a related but acceptable alternative, such as picking a fruit or snack they can have. Offering a choice empowers them and aligns with Montessori's focus on fostering independence.

- **Reflect Later.** Once the moment has passed, reflect on whether they were tired, hungry, or overstimulated. Adjusting the timing of outings or carrying a backup snack might help avoid similar situations in the future.

For You. It's okay to feel embarrassed or overwhelmed. Remind yourself that meltdowns are part of your child's learning process, not a sign of failure. Be kind to yourself, and know that every parent has been there.

Scenario 2. Artistic Chaos Turns to Frustration

You set up a painting activity for your child, envisioning a fun, creative moment, but within minutes, the paint is everywhere, and your toddler is howling because their picture "doesn't look right" and they "hate painting"

What to Do?

- **Validate Their Experience.** Say, "I see you worked hard on your picture, and it didn't turn out how you wanted. That can feel really frustrating." This helps your child feel seen and understood.

- **Shift the Focus to Exploration.** Gently remind them that art is about enjoying the process, not the outcome. Encourage them to explore textures and colors without worrying about perfection. Montessori emphasizes the joy of discovery and learning through hands-on activities.

- **Create a Safe Environment for Mess.** If the chaos feels overwhelming to you, consider setting up art activities outside. This way, both you and your toddler can relax more during the experience.

For You: It's normal to feel exasperated when a planned activity goes awry. Remind yourself that toddlers are still learning emotional regulation and fine motor control. Take a step back, focus on the moments of joy, and remember the bigger picture - you're fostering resilience as well as creativity.

Scenario 3. Power Struggles About Independence

Your toddler insists on putting on their shoes but gets frustrated when they can't manage it. They refuse help. This escalates into a meltdown, leaving you running late.

What to Do?

- **Acknowledge Their Effort.** Say, "I see you're trying so hard to put on your shoes by yourself. That's amazing!"

- **Offer Limited Help.** Montessori encourages independence, so offer just enough support without taking over. Try saying, "Would you like me to help with one shoe while you do the other?"

- **Plan Ahead.** To reduce frustration, allow extra time for activities where your toddler wants to assert independence. When you're in a rush, set the stage for success by choosing shoes that are easy to slip on, and offering practice time during calmer times.

For You: These moments can feel exasperating, especially when you're in a hurry. Remind yourself that your toddler's determination is a sign of healthy development, even if it's inconvenient. Take a deep breath and appreciate their budding independence.

Scenario 4. "I Hate You!"

One of the more heart-wrenching moments in parenting comes when your toddler, upset and frustrated, screams, "I hate you!" in response to being told "no" or when their demands aren't met. It can feel deeply personal and upsetting, but it's an important part of their emotional development.

What to Do:

- **Stay Calm and Acknowledge Their Feelings.** Remain composed and don't take the words personally. Kneel to their level, take a deep breath, and say, "I know you're really upset right now, and I understand you're feeling mad. It's okay to feel angry, but it's not okay to say hurtful words."

- **Set Boundaries with Empathy.** Gently reinforce boundaries by saying, "You can be mad at me, but it's not okay to say you hate me. We can talk about why you're upset and how we can solve this together."

- **Model Healthy Emotional Expression.** Use the moment to model how to express emotions in a healthier way. For example, "When I'm upset, I take a deep breath and say, 'I'm really angry.' Would you like to try that with me?"

- **Give Space if Needed.** Sometimes, your toddler may need a few minutes to calm down before they can engage in a conversation about their feelings. Let them know it's okay to take a break and try again when they're ready.

For You: It's normal to feel hurt or frustrated when your toddler uses such strong language. But remember, their brain is still developing, and they are learning how to express intense emotions. This is an opportunity to teach emotional regulation and empathy. Take a moment to center yourself and remind yourself that this is a phase.

Your toddler's love for you is unwavering, even if their words don't reflect that in the heat of the moment.

In short, setbacks aren't failures—they're opportunities to model patience, adaptability, and resilience. Your toddler is learning through trial and error, and so are you. By approaching these challenges with empathy and a willingness to adjust, you nurture your child's development while building a foundation of trust and connection.

Growth, Guidance and Gratitude

These precious toddler years are a time of rapid growth, transformation, and emotional discovery. Gentle parenting and Montessori principles offer a harmonious approach to navigating this stage, providing a solid foundation of empathy, respect, and independence.

Embracing these principles also supports your growth. You are learning to balance patience with flexibility, compassion with structure, and acceptance of imperfection with the joy of watching your child flourish.

The Montessori approach further encourages independence and problem-solving, allowing your child to explore, learn, and develop at their own pace in a safe and nurturing environment. By honoring your toddler's need for autonomy while maintaining clear boundaries, you support their growing sense of self and emotional regulation.

So, while the journey may present some challenges you hadn't expected, the rewards—seeing your child grow into a confident, independent, and emotionally aware individual—are immeasurable. Through gentle parenting and Montessori, you create a partnership with your child that honors their unique development while strengthening your unbreakable bond of love.

Reflective Questions

The transition from toddlerhood into early childhood is filled with leaps of independence, intense emotions, and occasional setbacks. As you reflect on this chapter, consider how your child's growth mirrors your own learning as a parent. The questions below are designed to help you think deeply about your responses, explore new strategies, and embrace a flexible, compassionate approach to this stage.

1. What recent interactions with peers has your child had, and what did they reveal about their emerging social skills?

2. Reflect on a time when your child demonstrated empathy—what did it teach you about their understanding of others' emotions?

3. How do you feel when your child frequently says "no," and what does that reaction reveal about your beliefs around authority and autonomy?

4. Reflect on a recent moment of conflict—how did you handle it, and what would you like to do differently next time?

5. How comfortable are you with allowing your child to make mistakes, and how do you respond when things don't go as expected?

6. How do you handle the messes or slower pace that come with fostering independence, and what mindset shifts could help you embrace the process?

7. What skills would you like to nurture over the next few months, and how can you create experiences to build them?

8. What role does screen time currently play in your household, and how does it align with your values and goals for your child?

9. Reflect on your current approach to collaborative play—what strategies have been most effective, and where could you use additional tools?

10. What emotions or assumptions come up for you around potty training, and how do they affect your approach?

11. Reflect on a recent challenge—how did you handle it, and what new strategies could you try in similar situations?

12. How do you model resilience in your own behavior, and how might that impact your child's response to challenges?

Chapter Five

Navigating Parenting Challenges

> *'Your child's behavior is not a referendum on your parenting.'* —E. Edlynn, PhD

Parenting with a gentle approach is a rewarding yet often demanding journey. As you embrace the principles of gentle parenting and incorporate Montessori methods, it's only natural that real-life challenges—such as doubt, fatigue, and frustration—can surface.

Despite your best efforts, there will be days when it feels as if the demands of gentle parenting are just too much. You may question your choices or feel uncertain about your approach. You're only human and these feelings are entirely normal. They don't diminish the positive impact of the approach you're striving to maintain. What's important is that you set realistic expectations and don't allow any setbacks to trigger feelings of guilt or inadequacy as a parent. Easier said than done, of course!

> *"In our talk, the journalist shared one example of using several gentle parenting tips to stop her two-year-old's undesirable behavior of jumping on a table. With no effect on his gleeful jumping, she finally yelled and took him off the table. She felt guilty for days."* —*Emily Edlynn.*

In this chapter, I want to address these very real doubts and fears and look at those times when you question the entire parenting approach. I will also provide some practical responses that will help you stay grounded, patient, and confident, even when things feel shaky.

Balancing Gentle Discipline with Real World Expectations

One of the toughest aspects of gentle parenting is the constant balancing act between empathy and the real-world pressures of daily life. There seems to be an expectation that you will maintain a perfect relationship with your child at all times.

The challenge lies in not internalizing every difficult moment as a reflection of our abilities or the quality of our connection with our child. In a recent article, author Emily Edlynn brings us back to reality and puts it in a nutshell.

> *"Sometimes kids are jerks. Sometimes we are jerks. We all have our moments. Every challenging behavior or meltdown does not need to be a referendum on our parenting or our relationship."*

Many parents, especially those who have decided to adopt a gentle parenting approach, feel a weighty responsibility to ensure that every interaction with their child is perfectly positive and nurturing. When their little one is upset, throws a tantrum, or refuses to cooperate, it can feel like a sign that something is wrong with the parenting style or the relationship itself.

It can be even more stressful when this behavior manifests in front of witnesses who may already be skeptical of our parenting approach. It's too easy to get caught in the trap of believing that our child's behavior reflects our success or failure as a parent. This mindset can lead to unnecessary guilt and frustration, making it harder to see things clearly.

Children are still developing the emotional and cognitive tools they need to navigate the world. When they act out, it's not necessarily a sign of a failed relationship or poor parenting. More likely it's simply part of their development at a given stage. So, it's important to be realistic, and most importantly, guilt-free, in how we respond.

To make this shift in mindset, it helps to have some practical strategies that encourage a more balanced approach to discipline.

Recognize Developmental Stages

Remind yourself that challenging behaviors are often linked to where your child is in their development. From ages 1-3, kids are learning emotional regulation, communication, and social boundaries. Their brains are still under construction, so their reactions to frustration or overstimulation might seem extreme or out of proportion. Just recognizing this can take away some of the pressure you feel to "fix" their behavior instantly.

Stay Calm, Stay Consistent

When a child resists, struggles with a limit, or has a meltdown, try to remain calm and composed. This doesn't mean suppressing your own emotion, but rather taking a moment to pause and respond thoughtfully - even if that means explaining that you are upset. Consistency in how you react - whether by setting a boundary or offering a gentle redirection—gives your child a sense of stability. But don't expect them to always act perfectly because they won't. Children will test boundaries, and that's a normal part of their development.

Practice Self-Compassion

> *"Toddlers are basically tiny philosophers, but instead of pondering, they just prove you're winging adulthood."* —@Nile Gomes, X, 11/23/24.

You don't have to be perfect. Remind yourself that every difficult moment doesn't require a perfect solution or perfect behavior from your little one. It's okay to acknowledge when you're frustrated or tired, and it's okay to take a break.

You don't need to be a calm, empathetic parent every second of the day. Sometimes, you'll need to step away to collect yourself or allow yourself to feel frustration. That's human. And your child will be okay if you do that.

Reframe "Failure" as "Learning"

If you or your child struggles to follow through with something— whether it's a new routine or learning to manage their emotions— it's helpful to reframe it as part of the learning process. Instead of feeling you've failed, see it as an opportunity for learning. So if your child resists potty training or refuses to follow a rule, don't beat yourself up. Instead, think of it as a learning opportunity for both of you. You'll deepen your understanding of your child's unique needs and temperament, and they'll learn more about the boundaries and expectations that help them feel safe.

Celebrate Progress, Not Perfection

While you're juggling the many demands of daily life, it's easy to get bogged down by moments of frustration or failure. But again, gentle parenting is about progress, not perfection. Celebrate the small victories—whether it's your child cooperating for a few minutes longer than usual, or you managing to stay calm in a tough situation. Each step forward, no matter how small, is a win.

By keeping things in perspective and accepting that neither you nor your child is perfect, you can approach parenting with more patience and less guilt. Guilt often arises from unrealistic expectations, and by acknowledging that challenging behaviors are a normal part of development, you can release the burden of constantly feeling like you're not doing enough.

Guide your child with empathy and connection, but recognize you need to be realistic with yourself. Parenting isn't about flawless interactions—it's about building a relationship that can withstand the bumps along the way. It's a journey with ups and downs, and as long as you stay connected to your child and practice patience, you're on the right path.

Resistance - Stay Calm and Redirect Gently

Resistance is an expected and natural part of early childhood development. When your child pushes back, whether by refusing to put on their shoes, clean up toys, or transition from play to mealtime, it's not a sign that you're failing as a parent or that your approach isn't working.

It's a sign that your child is learning to assert autonomy, explore boundaries, and express their preferences. Viewing these moments through a developmental lens can make all the difference in how you respond and how much pressure you put on yourself in these situations.

Let Go of Guilt

Children aged 1-3 are at a stage where their cognitive, emotional, and social abilities are still developing rapidly. Their brains are working hard to process emotions, learn new skills, and understand rules - all while managing impulses and testing limits. Resistance is often a sign of these internal processes at work. While they can be challenging to manage, remember that these moments are part of healthy development. Your child isn't trying to make life difficult; they're navigating their feelings and learning how to express them.

In a guilt-free approach to parenting, accept that resistance is not only normal but also an opportunity for growth—for both your child and yourself. Expecting perfect compliance from a toddler sets both of you up for frustration. Instead, aim to stay realistic and compassionate, knowing that resistance does not equal rebellion or disrespect; it's simply a learning phase.

Strategies to Help You Stay Calm and Redirect Gently

Pause Before Responding

When resistance flares, take a moment to pause and breathe. This quick pause helps you collect yourself and prevents a reactive response. Remaining calm models emotional regulation for your child and keeps the situation from escalating.

Empathize First

Acknowledge your child's feelings to show them you understand. Statements like, "I see that you don't want to stop playing right now. It's so much fun, isn't it?" can defuse tension and make your child feel heard. This step doesn't mean you're giving in -you're validating their emotions while preparing them for what comes next.

Offer Choices

Children at this age often crave some measure of control over their world. By providing limited choices, such as "Would you like to put on your shoes by yourself or with my help?" you empower them to take ownership of their actions. These choices help redirect their resistance into cooperation while still maintaining your boundaries.

Use Gentle Redirection

If your child is resisting an activity or refusing to follow a direction, try gentle redirection. This can involve turning the task into a game or engaging their imagination. For example, "Let's hop like bunnies to the table for lunch!" transforms a mundane moment into one filled with joy and play. Redirection doesn't mean avoiding the task; it's about guiding them in a way that aligns with their developmental need for play and exploration.

Keep Your Expectations Realistic

Understand that resistance won't vanish overnight, and it doesn't always mean your strategy isn't effective. Children will continue to test boundaries as they grow, and your role is to navigate these tests without guilt. Some days will go smoothly, and other days will be more challenging. Allow yourself to acknowledge when things don't go as planned, without blaming yourself or feeling defeated.

Staying Guilt-Free Through Challenging Moments

It's easy to fall into the trap of thinking that your child's resistance is a reflection of your shortcomings. But in reality, children are wired to push boundaries and assert their independence—it's part of their job as they develop. As a parent, your job is not to eliminate resistance but to guide them through it with understanding and patience.

When your efforts to stay calm and redirect don't work as well as you'd hoped, remind yourself that it's okay. Not every moment needs to be perfectly managed. There will be times when both you and your child are tired, frustrated, or just not at your best. In those moments, show yourself the same empathy you show your child.

Your goal is not flawless parenting but fostering a relationship where both of you feel safe navigating the ups and downs together.

Embracing Imperfection

Resistance doesn't mean your parenting approach is failing; it means your child is learning, growing, and becoming their own person. By staying calm, redirecting gently, and maintaining realistic expectations, you create an environment where your child can test limits safely, and you can parent with confidence—free from unnecessary guilt.

Parenting will always have moments of resistance, but each challenge is an opportunity to build trust, strengthen your bond, and grow alongside your child.

When You or Your Partner Struggle to Follow Through

Even with the best intentions, gentle parenting can be difficult to uphold consistently. Life stressors, exhaustion, and personal differences can lead to moments when one or both parents struggle to follow through with agreed-upon strategies.

These missteps don't mean failure—they are an integral part of the parenting journey. Understanding what happens when you or your partner go 'off-track' can help you approach these moments with empathy and regain your footing together.

When Follow-Through Falters

It's not uncommon for one parent to veer off the shared path, especially when emotions run high or there's a particularly stressful situation. Here's what can happen.

- Frustration Builds

  When one partner doesn't follow through with an agreed approach, it can create frustration for the other, leading to feelings of imbalance or disappointment. This can manifest in subtle signs such as clipped responses or a reluctance to participate in discipline. Meanwhile, the struggling partner may feel defensive or overwhelmed by their perceived lapse.

- Inconsistent Boundaries Create Mixed Signals

  From a child's perspective, inconsistency can be confusing. When boundaries aren't applied uniformly, children may begin to test limits to see where they truly stand. They might react by pushing further when one parent is more lenient, or by becoming more anxious when rules suddenly shift without explanation. This inconsistency can disrupt a child's sense of safety and predictability, leading to increased defiance or emotional outbursts as they navigate the uncertainty.

- Emotional Reactions

  Children are highly attuned to the emotional states of their parents. If a parent's struggle leads to raised voices or visible frustration, they may react in various ways. Sensitive children might withdraw or become fearful, while others might mirror the stress through louder protests, tantrums, or refusal to cooperate. They may start to associate discipline with tension rather than learning, which can erode trust over time.

- Behavioral Regression

  When children perceive inconsistency in responses, they may regress in behavior. For example, a child who previously responded well to gentle reminders might begin ignoring them or acting out in new ways. This can be their way of seeking clarity or attention, testing whether the boundaries are still secure, or craving reassurance when things feel unpredictable.

Getting Back on Track

Acknowledging these moments and finding ways to move forward as a team is essential. Here's how to realign after a misstep.

- **Recognize and Reflect**. Notice when you or your partner struggles to maintain consistency and reflect on what contributed to the lapse—whether it was fatigue, stress, or external pressures. Share these reflections openly, with an emphasis on understanding rather than blame. This transparency helps the child see that adults, too, learn and adapt, creating a model for resilience.

- **Check-In with Each Other and Your Child**. While checking in with your partner is essential, consider involving your child in age-appropriate ways if there has been noticeable confusion or stress. A simple "I know things felt different earlier, but we're all trying our best" can reassure them. Checking in with your partner-"I saw that was tough, how are you doing?" - can create a space for acknowledgment and shared problem-solving.

- **Reaffirm Your Shared Goals**. Reconnecting with your parenting philosophy helps not just you and your partner, but also stabilizes your child's environment. When parents realign and return to consistent boundaries, children regain a sense of predictability and security. Highlighting shared goals such as "We're here to help you learn safely" reinforces these messages.

- **Offer and Accept Support**. Supporting each other means stepping in without judgment. For example, if you see your partner struggling to maintain a calm tone, offering to take over can prevent situations from escalating. Similarly, accept help when you need a break. Your child learns teamwork and compassion by observing how parents support one another during difficult times.

- **Learn and Adapt**. Missteps offer insights into triggers and situations that need a different approach. Discuss what you both learned and agree on strategies that might work better next time. This proactive response not only prevents future missteps but shows children that learning from mistakes is valuable.

- **Maintain Empathy for Your Partner and Child**. Understand that children's behavior during inconsistent moments often reflects their attempt to make sense of the situation. Whether it's clinging more, pushing boundaries, or becoming upset, these are natural responses to perceived uncertainty. Offering empathy, rather than judgment, to your partner as they navigate this reality helps foster an environment where everyone feels supported.

Embracing Imperfection and Growth

When you or your partner struggle, it's easy to view these moments as setbacks. In reality, they are opportunities to model how to address challenges with compassion and commitment. By discussing the situation, adjusting, and moving forward together, you show your child that imperfections are part of life and that relationships grow stronger through understanding and shared effort. This process reinforces the idea that parenting is a partnership—an evolving journey where everyone, including your child, learns to navigate challenges with resilience and love.

Navigating the Challenges of Gentle Parenting

Adopting a gentle parenting approach, and enriching it with Montessori principles, is certainly not without its challenges. There will be moments of doubt, fatigue, and frustration - times when your child resists, when boundaries feel like they're slipping away, or when you and your partner struggle to stay on the same page. These moments are testing. They might even make you question whether this approach is truly the right fit for your family.

However, the benefits of sticking with it, and rooting your approach in understanding and empathy, are worth it in the long run. By creating a supportive, relationship-based foundation for your child's development, you help them build trust in themselves and the world around them.

And when you incorporate Montessori principles—encouraging independence, fostering problem-solving, and respecting the child's natural pace—you're equipping your child with the tools they need to navigate life's challenges confidently and resourcefully.

So even when things don't go according to plan, it's important to remember that every step you take toward emotional connection, empathetic listening, and gentle redirection brings lasting benefits. Over time, these practices help your child develop emotional intelligence, a love for learning, and the resilience needed to cope with adversity. Montessori encourages active participation in their learning, helping them develop a sense of autonomy and confidence that will serve them throughout their life.

In short, it's about doing the best you can in the moments you're in, and knowing that every time you model patience, consistency, and empathy, you're planting seeds for future growth. The storms of parenting a toddler will pass, but the relationship you're building with your child and the skills they're developing will last a lifetime.

So, even when the going gets tough, even if you're getting ready to throw in the towel, remind yourself that your commitment to gentle parenting and Montessori principles is worth every effort. The positive impact you're having now will ripple through your child's development, guiding them to become thoughtful, capable, and confident individuals.

In the end, the challenges you weather together will only strengthen the foundation you've built for your child's growth and your family's bond.

Reflective Questions

Parenting is a journey filled with unexpected challenges, and no approach is without its frustrations or missteps. This chapter explored the realities of staying calm, consistent, and compassionate in the face of resistance, fatigue, and societal pressures. The questions below encourage you to reflect on your personal struggles, celebrate your progress, and identify tools that will help you move forward with resilience and clarity.

1. When you feel frustrated or exhausted, what automatic thoughts or reactions tend to arise, and how do they affect your approach to gentle parenting?

2. What signals do you notice in your body or behavior when you are nearing burnout, and how do you typically respond?

3. What are some real-world situations where you've felt tension between gentle discipline and societal expectations, and how did you navigate them?

4. How do you differentiate between behavior that needs gentle redirection and actions that require more immediate intervention?

5. How do you manage public situations where your child's behavior doesn't meet others' expectations, and what inner dialogue could help you stay calm and focused?

6. What phrases or actions help you de-escalate tense situations while preserving your child's dignity?

7. How do you communicate with your partner about parenting struggles, and where could your communication improve?

8. Reflect on a recent moment when you didn't follow through on a parenting goal—what happened, and what did you learn?

9. How do you handle differences in parenting approaches between yourself and other caregivers, and how can you advocate for consistency?

10. What steps could you take to create a more supportive, aligned approach with your partner or other key caregivers?

11. How do you celebrate small wins and progress, even when perfection feels out of reach?

Chapter Six

Aligning Others with Your Parenting Approach

Parenting is never a solo endeavor—it's a team effort that extends beyond you and your child. Partners, grandparents, caregivers, and teachers all play vital roles in shaping your child's world. Yet, aligning your gentle parenting and Montessori-inspired approach with the perspectives of others can be challenging at times. Differing opinions, generational gaps, and deeply ingrained beliefs about what works best for children can create friction.

In this chapter, we'll consider strategies to foster understanding and collaboration with the key people in your child's life. These start with building a shared parenting style with your partner, emphasizing how to find common ground even when your approaches differ. Next, we'll address bridging generational divides with grandparents who may be used to a more traditional parenting style. We'll also look at ways to set clear, consistent expectations with caregivers and teachers, so your child receives the guidance they need in every environment.

Throughout, I'll share practical tips for overcoming resistance and misunderstandings - whether by picking your battles wisely, bringing people on board, or setting boundaries where necessary. By the end of this chapter, you'll have a toolkit to help you to align your parenting vision while respecting the individuality of those who support you on this journey.

Building Your Parenting Style with Your Partner.

Developing a shared parenting approach with your partner takes more than shared values—it requires thoughtful, detailed conversations and a commitment to understanding each other's perspectives. While overarching goals like "raising a kind child" or "encouraging independence" are helpful starting points, they need to be backed up by agreement on practical strategies for day-to-day parenting.

Genuine alignment goes beyond abstract concepts; it involves setting expectations for how to handle specific situations and creating a plan to navigate potential differences.

Start Conversations Early

If possible, begin discussing parenting strategies even before your baby is born. These conversations can be part of the anticipation and excitement of expecting a child, while also fostering growth and closeness as a couple. Early discussions can help identify where you align and where you might diverge in your approaches.

For example, one partner might believe in letting a toddler "cry it out" for sleep training, while the other feels strongly about responding immediately to any cries by picking up and soothing the little one. By mapping out these "red lines" in advance, you set the stage for smoother navigation when real challenges arise.

Identify Areas of Alignment

To find common ground, go beyond vague aspirations and talk through specific aspects of parenting. For example, create a list of areas to cover, ensuring that both of you are clear on expectations.

- **Discipline Methods**. Will you use time-ins, time-outs, logical consequences, or focus exclusively on positive reinforcement?

- **Emotional Responses**. How will you both react to tantrums? Or shyness, reticence? Or unwillingness to share? Or aggression towards siblings or playmates? Is one of you more inclined to take a calm, empathetic approach while the other tends to get frustrated more quickly? Discuss strategies for staying patient and redirecting calmly.

- **Screen Time**. What are your boundaries regarding television, tablets, or phones? Do you agree on what age to introduce these and how long they should be used? What guidelines will you agree to in respect of your own screentime when your child is present?

- **Sleep Training**. What methods are you comfortable using? Will you follow a gentle, co-sleeping approach, or do you lean toward structured sleep training?

- **Nutrition and Eating Habits**. How will you handle meals, snacks, and potential picky eating? Will you enforce "finish your plate" rules or take a more relaxed approach that respects a child's appetite and preferred foods?

- **Routines and Schedules**. Will you both agree on establishing a daily routine, or is one partner more comfortable with spontaneous, child-led activities?

- **Encouraging Independence**. How do you plan to implement Montessori principles such as allowing a child to dress themselves or help with simple household chores? Are you both prepared for the patience this requires?

- **Safety and Risk-Taking**. How do you both feel about letting a toddler explore and take small, managed risks? Discussing comfort levels here can help avoid misunderstandings when supervising activities.

Identifying Opportunities to Compromise

In some areas, you may find it necessary to adopt the same approach to provide consistency, such as in discipline and emotional responses. Children thrive on predictability, so mixed messages can cause confusion. For other areas, you might "agree to disagree." For example, if one partner enjoys messy or 'wild' play while the other prefers structured activities, allowing each partner to engage with the child in their own way can enrich the child's experiences and help you each get the most fun from playtimes.

> Keep in mind that mutually supportive relationships are more important than our various likes/dislikes and opinions, so make sure you don't choose a frivolous hill to take a stand and die on.

Keep the wise words of Ralph Waldo Emerson in mind. *"For every minute you are angry, you lose sixty seconds of happiness."*

> If you really can't agree, and the topic is something either of you are unable to compromise on, consider asking for help from an impartial third party. Remember that modeling a healthy relationship - including productive and respectful ways to resolve disputes - is part of your gentle parenting approach.

Developing an "On the Same Page" Strategy

Once you've discussed and identified any points of divergence, the next step is to work out how you're going to respond when differences arise. Here are some practical tips to help you stay on the same parenting page.

- **Have Regular Check-Ins**. Make it a habit to talk weekly or monthly about what's working and what isn't. This helps you address concerns or areas of friction before they escalate.

- **Tag Team When Needed**. If one partner is struggling in the moment, agree that the other will step in with support, whether through words of encouragement or taking over for a few minutes.

- **Create a Signal for "Pause"**. Decide on a way to signal when you need to pause a discussion or recalibrate your response to a situation—especially when emotions run high.

- **Offer Non-Judgmental Support**. If your partner's approach isn't what you would choose, avoid critiquing in the moment. Discuss adjustments or compromises later, in a calm, understanding manner.

- **Share Responsibility**. Recognize that both partners contribute to successes and setbacks. Avoid making one person the default "disciplinarian" or "comforter."

Navigating Real-Life Scenarios

Imagine a moment when your toddler is in full meltdown mode over refusing to put on shoes and the family needs to be on the move. You might be ready to wait them out, acknowledging their feelings and offering empathy, while your partner's instinct is to take a firmer stance (or vice versa!). To avoid undermining each other, establish beforehand that if one approach doesn't seem to work, you will switch to the other's method as a unified front.

Finding common ground with your partner is essential for creating a consistent, loving environment for your child. The work involved in aligning your approaches, discussing expectations, and refining them over time reinforces your shared commitment to the parenting journey. When disagreements occur—and they will—it's not a sign of failure but an opportunity to strengthen your teamwork and deepen your understanding of each other's perspectives.

Getting Grandparents on Board

> *Because [grandparents] are usually free to love and guide and befriend the young without having to take daily responsibility for them, they can often reach out past pride and fear of failure and close the space between generations." —President Jimmy Carter.*

Grandparents play an invaluable role in a child's life, offering love, wisdom, and a deep sense of connection to family heritage. Whatever their age or generation, they bring a wealth of life experience that can help you - after all, they have already navigated the exhaustion, stress, and doubts that come with raising children. While there may be some generational differences in parenting styles, most grandparents are eager to step in and support, especially when they see their children becoming parents themselves.

Understanding and Respecting Their Experience

> *"If I had known how wonderful it would be to have grandchildren, I'd have had them first." —Lois Wyse.*

Grandparents often draw on their own successful parenting experiences and may be confident that their ways worked best - after all, look how well you turned out! Memories of their own struggles will have faded over time (as yours will, too).

When they see you trying a new approach, it's essential to help them realize that this shift is not a criticism aimed at them, but rather a reflection of evolving research and a style that suits your personality. Inviting them to share their experiences as part of the learning process will help foster a spirit of collaboration rather than division.

Balancing Old and New Approaches

While your parenting style may incorporate elements such as gentle discipline or Montessori-based independence, it's important to recognize that your parents' approaches likely developed in a different context.

If you are fortunate enough to have your own parents on hand to help guide you through the challenges of those early years, and to share the joys, there are immeasurable benefits for the whole family.

> *"Nobody can do for little children what grandparents do. Grandparents sort of sprinkle stardust over the lives of little children." —Alex Haley.*

Grandparents are typically brimming over with love for the little one - and pride in the new parent they raised so successfully (yes, that's you!).

Having left the responsibilities of raising small children in the distant past, they will want to understand your view of what's best for their grandchildren and be willing to adapt when they see its benefits.

> *"As you are now, so once were we." —James Joyce.*

At the same time, they'll be eager to pass on their child-rearing wisdom and help you avoid any mistakes they believe they made - so take the time to listen as they regale you with their experiences.

Sharing your approach and comparing strategies openly, perhaps by demonstrating how you guide your child through challenging moments, can make grandparents feel included and more prepared to offer support.

Consistency and Clear Expectations

When grandparents play an active role as babysitters or caregivers, consistency in your child's routine becomes even more crucial. Start on the right foot by communicating clear guidelines for handling specific situations, such as meals, play, and discipline.

For example, if you prefer that your toddler not have sweets before lunch, express this boundary clearly. Let grandparents know it's about establishing healthy habits, not about withholding treats altogether.

To help them feel confident in resisting moments of peak toddler persuasion, try these steps.

- **Emphasize Your Trust.** Let them know you trust their judgment and value their help. This can make them more inclined to respect your guidelines.

- **Provide Context.** Explain why certain rules, like avoiding sweets before lunch, matter for your child's routine and well-being.

- **Reinforce Boundaries Together.** Discuss how they might handle the situation when your child asks for sweets. Suggest responses that align with your approach, such as offering an alternative or redirecting the child's attention to something else.

- **Be Open to Their Ideas.** Having learned to resist your pleading when you were a child, grandparents may well be able to offer suggestions for managing these types of situations. Including their input helps bridge understanding and respect, so be ready to learn from the pros.

Addressing Over-Indulgence

It's inevitable, though, that despite their best efforts, grandparents might sometimes give in to your toddler's pitiful pleas for sweets, cookies or other treats. If this happens, avoid viewing it as a major setback. Understand that their desire to indulge your little one comes from a place of love and a wish to see their grandchildren happy. Approach the situation with empathy, emphasizing that occasional lapses are part of the learning process for everyone.

Consider saying something like, "I know [name] can be persistent, and it's hard to say no when they're looking at you with those big eyes. We're just trying to keep certain routines in place, so maybe next time we can come up with a shared way to handle those requests."

Building a Supportive Partnership

> "When your mother asks, 'Do you want a piece of advice?' it's a mere formality. It doesn't matter if you answer yes or no. You're going to get it anyway."
> —Erma Bombeck.

To maintain harmony, remember that your parents and in-laws are allies who want the best for their grandchildren. Rather than focusing on differences, emphasize shared values, such as creating a nurturing, loving environment. By showing that you appreciate their involvement and value their support, you create a foundation where everyone is working toward the same goal. raising a happy, confident child.

Reinforce their important role with positive feedback and celebrate moments when they embrace your parenting style. This helps build a strong team where grandparents feel respected and trusted, ensuring that their support continues to be an incredible source of reassurance and strength for you as a parent.

Setting Clear Expectations with Caregivers and Teachers

When it comes to your child's care and education outside the home—whether this involves babysitters, nannies, daycare providers, or teachers—it's important to ensure consistent guidance and alignment with your parenting approach

While each caregiver brings their own unique skills and perspectives, clear communication from the get-go and mutual respect are key to creating a supportive, unified environment for your child. The goal is not to control, but to collaborate, so that everyone is on the same page in supporting your child's growth and well-being.

Start with Clear Communication

Before sending your child off to daycare or entrusting them to a caregiver, take the time to have an open conversation about your parenting philosophy and the approach you're using at home. Whether you're implementing gentle discipline, Montessori methods, or other child-centered practices, make sure caregivers understand the basics and why they're important to you and your child.

For example, if you're working on building independence and giving your child choices, explain how that looks in practice—whether it's letting them decide between two shirt options or offering simple choices at mealtimes. If your approach involves setting gentle boundaries and redirecting behavior instead of using punishment, make sure caregivers know what that looks like as well.

This discussion doesn't need to be overly detailed, but it's essential to provide context so caregivers understand your priorities and approach. You can say things like, "We're focusing on helping [name] make choices as part of a growing sense of independence," or, "We use redirection instead of punishment to guide behavior."

Provide Practical Guidelines for Consistency

Consistency across different environments is important to help children feel secure and supported. Set specific expectations for how your child's needs should be met in practical, everyday situations.

- **Behavior Management**. Discuss how to handle behavioral issues in ways that align with your values. For example, if your child struggles with sharing, explain your approach to managing conflicts. "When [name] refuses to share, we ask them to use their words and express how they feel, then help them find a solution. We prefer not to use time-outs, but redirection or offering a different activity."

- **Meal and Snack Times**. Let caregivers know about any dietary preferences, restrictions, or routines that matter to you. If your child has specific eating habits (e.g., no sugary snacks before lunch), make sure they understand and agree to those boundaries. You can say, "We try to stick to a routine of eating a balanced lunch before any treats, so please help reinforce that."

- **Nap and Bedtime Routines**. If your child has a specific nap or bedtime routine that's important for them to feel settled, let caregivers know how they can help. For example, "We use a calming bedtime routine with books and soft music to help [child's name] wind down. It's important that this stays consistent even when we're not there."

Keep Lines of Communication Open

When working with caregivers, set up an open line of communication. Encourage them to ask questions and share their observations about how your child is doing in their care. Likewise, make sure they feel comfortable providing feedback to you. This ensures that if something isn't working, or if there's a situation you're unaware of, it can be addressed in a timely and constructive way.

For instance, you might say, "I'd love to hear how they're adjusting in the classroom. Are there any behaviors you've noticed that we should work on at home?" This fosters an environment of collaboration and shows that you value their input while maintaining open and respectful communication.

Addressing Differences in Approach

Sometimes, caregivers may approach situations differently, either because of their personal experiences or training. This doesn't always mean they're wrong, so try to find ways to align their approach with yours for consistency. If you notice any discrepancies, talk about them respectfully and constructively.

For example, if a caregiver uses a strategy that doesn't fit with your approach, for example, offering a reward for positive behavior, calmly explain why that might not be effective for your child's development, but remember that collaboration is a two-way street.

While you should communicate your expectations clearly, it's equally important to be receptive to the caregiver's ideas and feedback. They have valuable insights into your child's behavior outside the home, and their perspective can help you better understand your child's needs in different settings.

Making it a Partnership

By setting clear expectations, communicating openly, and being willing to adapt when necessary, you'll be creating a positive, collaborative relationship with caregivers and teachers. This partnership is key to providing your child with a consistent, nurturing environment that aligns with the gentle parenting principles you value, helping them thrive both at home and in other settings.

Once again, let's be clear that creating a unified approach between home and outside caregivers doesn't require perfection, but rather a willingness to work together as a team. When everyone involved in your child's care understands and respects your parenting approach, it allows your child to feel safe, supported, and confident in all environments.

Overcoming Resistance and Misunderstandings

We've all heard the saying that it takes a village. Parenting is a collaborative effort, and as much as you may have a clear idea of how you want to raise your child, it's inevitable that others will be involved.

From your partner to extended family members and caregivers, the people around you play a crucial role in supporting or guiding your child. Naturally, this can create friction when different parenting styles or perspectives come into play. Navigating these differences in a way that respects your approach while maintaining harmonious relationships can be challenging, but it's an essential part of creating a supportive environment for your child's growth.

Understanding Resistance

Resistance to your parenting style can manifest in many ways. Maybe your partner doesn't fully align with your approach to discipline, or your in-laws think you're being too lenient with your child.

Sometimes, it's more subtle—an offhand comment here, a well-meaning suggestion there, or a little pushback when you leave your child in someone else's care. While this resistance can be frustrating, it's also natural. People around you have their own experiences, beliefs, and fears about what's best for the child, and it can take time for them to adjust to new ways of thinking or doing things.

The key to overcoming resistance isn't to force everyone to adopt your style right away, but to create space for understanding. Begin by explaining the values that guide your parenting decisions. Rather than presenting your approach as a criticism of others, focus on the positive outcomes you've observed—how your child is thriving emotionally, or how your approach strengthens your relationship with them.

This way, you're not trying to "prove" that your way is right; you're sharing a perspective and inviting others to be part of your parenting team.

Communicating Boundaries and Setting Guidelines

When it comes to your child's care, there will be certain non-negotiables—boundaries you feel strongly about. Whether it's screen time, food choices, or discipline methods, these are the areas where consistency matters, especially if your child will spend time with others. Clear communication is essential to ensure your boundaries are respected without creating unnecessary tension.

- **Be Clear and Specific**. Rather than vague guidelines, get into specifics. For example, "We try to limit screen time to 30 minutes a day, and we don't provide sugary snacks before meals." The more specific you can be about expectations, the easier it will be for others to comply.

- **Explain the 'Why'**. People are more likely to respect guidelines when they understand the reasoning behind them. Share why these rules are important to you and your child's well-being, whether it's for better sleep, healthier habits, or emotional security.

- **Make It Collaborative**. Set boundaries in a way that involves others in the process. Instead of simply dictating, say something like, "We've found this routine really works well for us, but I'm open to hearing your thoughts. What do you think might work here?" This invites others to engage with your approach rather than dismiss it.

- **Respectful Pushback**. If someone disregards a boundary or guideline, address it promptly but respectfully. Use it as an opportunity for discussion, not confrontation. For example, if your child is given a sugary snack before lunch, gently remind the caregiver of your rule and reiterate its importance.

Using Resistance as a Shared Learning Opportunity

One of the biggest challenges in having others involved in your child's life is that different people bring different styles to the table. For example, grandparents may spoil your child with affection and indulgences, which can conflict with your more structured approach. Caregivers might have their own ideas about how to handle discipline, or perhaps a friend might suggest a different routine than the one you've established. These moments can be tricky to navigate, but it's important to approach them with flexibility and understanding.

Rather than viewing differences as a problem to be solved, approach them as an opportunity to see things from another perspective. Sometimes, this means stepping back and letting others take the lead—especially with grandparents who may feel their experience gives them the authority to offer advice. Let them be involved in a way that doesn't feel like you're micromanaging. However, if you observe something that doesn't align with your guidelines or values, calmly address it, focusing on the child's best interests rather than criticizing anyone's approach.

In these situations, it's important to allow people to be themselves, but to keep your child's well-being front and center. And remember, you don't need to "win" every parenting discussion. In some cases, agreeing to a flexible, middle-ground solution can be more productive than enforcing your stance rigidly.

The Importance of Patience and Empathy

Building a strong, supportive team around your child is an essential aspect of both gentle parenting and the Montessori approach. Both emphasize respect—for your child's needs, for their individuality, and for the contributions of others involved in their life. Just as you aim to guide your child with empathy and understanding, extending those same values to the adults who share in your parenting journey can create a cohesive, nurturing environment where your child can thrive.

Open communication is your most powerful tool in this process. Explaining your perspective—why gentle parenting principles or Montessori techniques are important to you—can help others see the value in your approach. Patience is key. People may not immediately understand or agree, especially if their experiences with parenting differ significantly. Yet over time, consistent, respectful conversations can bridge these divides.

Flexibility also plays a crucial role. Recognizing that others may have valid insights, even if their style differs, allows you to bring them into your child's support system without forcing conformity. This balance between setting clear guidelines and respecting others' contributions strengthens relationships and builds a broader network of care for your child.

Aligning others with your parenting approach requires emotional resilience. The process can be as rewarding as it is challenging, and the energy it takes cannot be underestimated. To remain effective, present, and consistent in your parenting, self-care is not just helpful—it's essential.

In the next chapter, we'll focus on why prioritizing your own well-being is foundational to gentle parenting. You'll learn practical strategies for avoiding burnout, recognizing when you need a break, and fostering harmony in your relationships, ensuring that you and your family continue to grow together.

Reflective Questions

Parenting often requires alignment and collaboration with those who play a key role in your child's life—whether that's a partner, grandparents, or caregivers. This chapter explored how to find common ground, address differences, and set clear expectations to create a supportive, unified approach. Use the questions below to help you reflect on your relationships with those who influence your child's development, enabling you to strengthen communication, overcome misunderstandings, and build a nurturing team approach.

1. How do you and your partner approach parenting differently, and how do these differences reflect your own upbringings?

2. How do you feel when you or your partner struggle to maintain consistency with gentle parenting, and how do you typically respond?

3. How do you communicate with your partner about parenting struggles, and where could your communication improve?

4. How do you approach conversations with grandparents about your parenting choices, especially when they disagree with your approach?

5. How do you maintain respect for the grandparents' experience while asserting your own parenting choices and needs?

6. What are the key parenting values you want caregivers or teachers to be aware of when interacting with your child, and how do you communicate these?

7. How do you ensure consistency in discipline and guidance between your home and other caregivers, such as teachers or babysitters?

8. Reflect on a time when you encountered resistance from a partner, caregiver, or teacher regarding your parenting choices. How did you handle it, and what did you learn from the experience?

9. What steps can you take to ensure that your child feels comfortable and supported in all settings, even when the approaches may vary slightly?

10. What boundaries do you need to set with others who may not respect your parenting style, and how can you assert them while maintaining positive relationships?

Chapter Seven

The Foundation of Gentle Parenting - Your Well-Being

> *"You are worth the quiet moment. You are worth the deeper breaths and the time it takes to slow down, be still, and rest."* —*Morgan Harper Nichols.*

Parenting young children is no small feat. Between the sleepless nights, endless snack requests, and finding Cheerios in places you didn't think they could ever be wedged, it's easy to feel like you're running on fumes.

Gentle parenting calls for patience, empathy, and the kind of energy that would rival a marathon runner's. But there's a catch. you can't pour from an empty cup—or, in parenting terms, you can't nurture your child when you're completely drained.

Self-care isn't some luxury reserved for spa weekends or dreamy solo vacations. It's about finding practical, doable ways to recharge so you can bring your best self to your parenting. Yes, the stressors will still be there—the spilled milk, the tantrums, the never-ending "But why?" questions—but how you handle them depends on how well you've taken care of yourself. When you feel balanced, it's easier to respond with calm and clarity instead of snapping like a dry twig.

> *"Talk to yourself like you would to someone you love."*
> —Brené Brown.

And don't forget - your child is watching you like a tiny hawk. They're learning from you, even when you're not actively teaching. How you handle stress, take breaks, and prioritize your needs sends them an important message about resilience and self-respect. By showing them that it's okay—and necessary—to take care of yourself, you're giving them a blueprint for a healthy, balanced life.

When you're rested and recharged, you're better equipped to connect with your child in meaningful ways. You'll find it easier to respond with thoughtfulness instead of frustration, to be present even when the day feels chaotic.

In this chapter, we'll consider the why and how of self-care, with practical tips for weaving it into your life, recognizing the signs of burnout, and maintaining healthy relationships while navigating the beautiful (and messy) demands of gentle parenting and nurturing that twist of Montessori-inspired independence.

Burnout Ahead. Spot the Signs and Stop the Spiral

Gentle parenting is all about patience, empathy, and connection— but let's be honest, it can also be exhausting. Add in the rest of life's demands, and it's no wonder so many parents feel like they're running on empty. The good news? Catching burnout before it fully takes over can help you stay grounded and present for your family.

The Many Demands on Your Time

Parenting doesn't happen in a vacuum. It's a delicate dance of juggling your child's needs, your own responsibilities, and everything life throws at you. Here's what you're up against.

Childcare Responsibilities

Parenting young children can feel like an endless loop of putting out fires. Soothe the crying baby. Tame the toddler tantrum. Answer the "why is the sky blue?" question for the fifth time today. While these moments can be meaningful, they also pile up. The expectation to stay attentive 24/7 is overwhelming, and when you inevitably fall short, it's easy to spiral into guilt.

Work Commitments

Whether you work in an office, from home, or as a full-time parent, the transition from "work mode" to "parent mode" is brutal. One minute you're wrapping up a meeting or folding laundry; the next, you're refereeing sibling arguments or trying to cook dinner while helping with homework. The constant gear-shifting takes a toll, leaving you wondering how anyone keeps up without a magic wand (spoiler. no one does).

School and Daycare Schedules

Keeping up with drop-offs, pickups, and random schedule changes can feel like an Olympic event. Then there are the curveballs. a sick kid, a surprise closure, or the dreaded "costume day" announcement you find at 10 p.m. The unpredictability can leave you frazzled, making it harder to approach parenting with the calm you aspire to.

Household Responsibilities

Let's face it: the laundry pile isn't folding itself, and the dishes don't take holidays. The relentless cycle of cooking, cleaning, and general chaos management can leave you feeling like you're treading water. Without a moment to catch your breath, even minor hiccups can feel like monumental challenges.

> *"Cleaning your house while your kids are still growing up is like shoveling the walk before it stops snowing."*
> —Phyllis Diller

Pressure from External Expectations

It's not just the internal voice whispering "do better" that wears you down—it's also the world watching. Social media, family, friends. they all seem to demand a picture-perfect parent who's calm, composed, and crushing it. The truth is, nobody's life looks like that behind the scenes, but the pressure to keep up appearances is real and exhausting.

Strategies to Help You Recharge and Reset

Preventing burnout isn't about overhauling your life overnight; it's about small, consistent changes that restore balance. Here are some strategies to try.

Prioritize Your Rest

Sleep isn't a luxury—it's essential for physical and emotional well-being. But for many parents, long stretches of uninterrupted sleep can feel impossible. That's where alternative rest strategies can help.

One such practice is **Non-Sleep Deep Rest (NSDR)**. This simple, guided method involves lying down, closing your eyes, and following a relaxation protocol, such as yoga nidra or focused breathing exercises. NSDR sessions can last as little as 10-20 minutes and have been shown to improve focus, reduce stress, and even mimic some of the restorative benefits of sleep. By incorporating NSDR into your day—even during your child's nap or after bedtime—you can give your body and mind a much-needed recharge.

Additionally, it's worth rethinking your bedtime routine. Are late-night chores or screen time eating into your rest? Consider setting a firm "wind-down" time in the evening to signal to your body that it's time to relax. Small changes, like dimming lights, reading a calming book, or practicing mindfulness, can make falling asleep easier and improve the quality of your rest.

Simplify Your Schedule

The idea that parents—especially mothers—should excel at multitasking is both outdated and exhausting. Switching between multiple tasks may feel efficient, but it drains your mental energy and often leaves you feeling scattered. Instead, focus on single-tasking whenever possible. For example, give yourself permission to ignore the laundry pile while playing with your child or leave emails unread until nap time.

Look for ways to trim non-essential tasks from your routine. Do you really need to bake from scratch for every school event? Can errands be combined or delegated? Scaling back your to-do list frees up precious energy to spend on what truly matters.

Ask for Help

Many parents hesitate to ask for help, whether out of pride, guilt, or the belief that they should be able to "handle it all." But sharing the load doesn't mean you're failing; it means you're human. Start small. ask a friend to watch your child for an hour, or let your partner take over a bedtime routine. Being open about your needs not only lightens your burden but also models for your children that it's okay to seek support.

Build Mini-Breaks Into Your Day

> *"Almost everything will work again if you unplug it for a few minutes, including you." —Anne Lamott.*

Even a few minutes to yourself can make a big difference. Step outside for fresh air, do a short mindfulness exercise, or simply sit quietly with a cup of tea. Avoid the temptation to use these moments to catch up on tasks—true breaks are about rest, not productivity.

Stay Connected to Joy

Parenting is demanding, but it's vital to nurture your sense of self beyond that role. Research suggests that engaging in activities you find meaningful or enjoyable can buffer against stress and improve overall well-being.

Here are some strategies to reconnect with joy.

- **Practice Gratitude.** Taking a few moments each day to reflect on what you're grateful for can shift your perspective and boost your mood. Consider keeping a journal or sharing your gratitude aloud with your family.

- **Rediscover Your Passions.** Think about hobbies or interests you've set aside and carve out time to revisit them, even if only for a short while each week. Creative outlets like painting, writing, or gardening can be deeply restorative.

- **Move Your Body.** Exercise doesn't have to mean a full workout. A walk around the block, a quick dance session in the kitchen, or gentle stretching can release endorphins and improve your energy levels.

- **Connect With Others.** Strong social connections are linked to greater resilience and happiness. Make time for friends or join a community group where you can share experiences and feel supported.

Reclaiming joy is about finding what works for you and integrating it into your life in manageable ways. When you feel fulfilled, you're better equipped to handle the challenges of parenting with patience and empathy.

Fill Your Cup While Filling Theirs

Of course, the goal is to avoid burnout in the first place. Finding time for self-care as a parent of young children might feel like chasing a mirage—enticing but always out of reach. Yet, even small steps can help you recharge, and they're essential for maintaining the patience and empathy that gentle parenting relies on. Here are some ideas about how to integrate self-care into your daily life without it feeling like one more thing on your already packed to-do list.

Individual Self-Care Practices

Call Out to Your Village. Whether it's a grandparent, a friend, or a trusted neighbor, let others step in when they can. A short break - just long enough to savor a cup of tea or enjoy a quick walk - can work wonders. Don't let guilt convince you that you have to do it all; your support system is there for a reason - and they know that reason is to help you when you need help.

Micro-Breaks Add Up. Big blocks of free time may be an unattainable luxury, but short bursts of rest can still make a difference. While your child naps or engages in independent play, take five minutes to breathe deeply, stretch, or sit with a calming podcast. Even a tiny pause can reset your mind.

Multitask with Joy. If your day is a whirlwind of chores, bring some positivity into the mix. Listen to music that makes you smile or an audiobook you've been meaning to catch up on. Instead of viewing these moments as drudgery, think of them as an opportunity to sprinkle in some happiness.

Say Yes to Help. Asking for help can feel awkward—like admitting you can't handle everything. But here's the truth: nobody can. Handing off tasks to a partner, friend, or family member doesn't mean you're falling short. It means you're human and wise enough to prioritize your well-being.

From Surviving to Thriving - Together

By prioritizing your well-being as a team, and ensuring you stay alert to the health of your partnership, you not only strengthen your connection but also create a more supportive and harmonious foundation for your family.

Take Turns and Share the Load. Effective teamwork means making sure both partners get a breather. Divide parenting duties so one of you can enjoy some uninterrupted downtime. A little planning can go a long way toward preventing resentment or burnout.

Make Time for Mini-Dates. Waiting for a grand, romantic evening might mean waiting forever. Instead, find small moments to reconnect—a quiet coffee together, a stroll around the block, or even just 15 minutes chatting after the kids are asleep. These brief interludes can remind you why you're such a great team.

Be Honest About Needs. It's easy to assume your partner knows what you're thinking, but clear communication makes everything simpler. Talk about what you each need to feel balanced, whether it's an hour to exercise, a nap, or a little quiet time. Supporting each other creates a healthier home for everyone.

Finding Balance

Let Perfection Go. Your home doesn't have to be spotless, and not every meal needs to be Pinterest-worthy. Recognize what truly matters and ease up on the rest. Kids don't remember how tidy the living room was—they remember the giggles during a pillow fight or the stories before bed.

Celebrate Wins—Even the Small Ones. Maybe you kept your cool during a tantrum or found time to read a chapter of your favorite book. Acknowledge those moments. Celebrating little victories builds confidence and reminds you of the progress you're making.

Stay Connected to You. When possible, schedule a regular "you" activity, such as joining a book club, attending a hobby class, or scheduling a manicure, to remind yourself of who you are beyond parenting.

Maintaining a Healthy Partnership Amid Parenting Challenges

The demands of parenting can put strain on even the strongest relationships, but your partnership doesn't have to take a backseat. Shifting the focus to nurturing your connection—rather than just managing parenting struggles—helps you both feel supported, valued, and more capable of handling the journey together.

Here are a few practical suggestions to get you thinking of creative ways to maintain your close partnership while managing the demands of parenthood.

Prioritize Your Emotional Connection

After a long day of managing the kids, exhaustion can make it easy to simply collapse into bed without much communication. Instead, intentionally set aside time each evening for emotional check-ins. For example, after the kids go to bed, sit down together and ask, "What was the best part of your day?" and "What was the hardest part?" This goes beyond surface-level conversation and helps both partners connect emotionally.

Additionally, share something vulnerable, such as a worry you're carrying, or stress from your day—this fosters emotional closeness even in the midst of exhaustion.

Set Clear Boundaries and Expectations

Parenting doesn't come with a manual, but without clear expectations, frustrations build quickly. Start by having a weekly conversation to review and align on priorities and schedules. For example, if one partner has a big work project and the other is managing child care, agree in advance on specific tasks each person will take on.

Also, create boundaries around personal time—such as a set "me-time" each week where one partner gets an hour of alone time to recharge. Explicitly stating that this time is non-negotiable avoids future resentments and helps you both avoid burnout.

Share Decision-Making Responsibility

Decision-making should be an ongoing, shared process between partners, not just about chores but about the bigger picture. For example, when making choices about child care, school decisions, or family finances, sit down together regularly (e.g., once a month) to discuss these topics.

Take turns bringing up any concerns or ideas, and make sure both your opinions are heard. This could mean co-developing a monthly budget, talking about your child's development or behavior patterns together, and deciding on actions to take, ensuring both partners have equal involvement.

Cultivate a Shared Vision for Your Family

When life gets hectic, it's easy to lose sight of your shared values. Establish a family mission statement that helps you both stay grounded. For example, you could say, "We want our children to grow up in a home filled with patience and understanding." Having a clear vision helps you both make decisions in alignment with your values, especially when stressors arise. If parenting becomes overwhelming, revisit this vision together to remind yourselves of your collective purpose and goals.

Regularly Reassess Your Needs

As your parenting evolves, so do your needs as individuals and as a couple. Schedule regular "relationship check-ins" (every 2–3 months) where you review not only how you're managing the responsibilities of parenting, but how you're meeting each other's personal needs.

This could be as simple as asking, "Do you feel like you're getting enough time for yourself?" or "What support do you need more of?" These check-ins create space for honest, open conversations and prevent long-term dissatisfaction or burnout.

Foster Intimacy Beyond the Bedroom

Intimacy doesn't just happen in the bedroom—it thrives in everyday moments. Make time for intimate moments throughout the day, even if it's just a small gesture like holding hands while you're cooking dinner or sharing a quick kiss in the morning.

If circumstances allow, set aside one evening a week (e.g., a "date night") where you leave the kids with a sitter or family member and do something that connects you beyond the parenting role. It could be a quiet walk, a favorite meal, or watching a movie together. Intimacy doesn't require grand gestures—it's about consistent, thoughtful connection.

Pay Attention to Nonverbal Communication

Your body language can say more than words. When parenting gets stressful, small signals like crossed arms or a tense voice can communicate frustration, even if you don't mean to. Practice being mindful about your nonverbal cues—when speaking to your partner, make eye contact, maintain an open posture, and use a calm tone of voice. Even small physical gestures like a pat on the back or a reassuring touch can communicate empathy and understanding, reinforcing emotional closeness during stressful times.

Build Resilience Together

Viewing parenting challenges as opportunities for growth can strengthen your bond. When difficulties arise, tackle them as a team. For instance, if your child is going through a difficult phase, instead of one person feeling solely responsible, work together to come up with a plan.

Discuss strategies for handling behavior and parenting approaches, then check in regularly to assess what's working. Sharing the burden of inevitable challenges prevents anyone from feeling alone and helps reinforce your resilience as a couple.

Seek Professional Support When Needed

Sometimes, despite best efforts, couples need external help. If you feel something is going very wrong, don't wait for problems to escalate before seeking professional support.

For example, if you're feeling stuck in communication or constant conflict, consider seeing a therapist who specializes in couples counseling. Therapy can provide tools for better communication, conflict resolution, and emotional support. Proactively seeking help not only shows commitment to your relationship, but it also sets a positive example for your children about healthy ways to handle stress and resolve conflict.

Caring for Yourself

Parenting is challenging, and the physical and emotional demands can quickly deplete your energy. To stay resilient and avoid burnout, it's important to apply the principles of gentle parenting and Montessori to yourself and those close to you.

So, be kind to yourself. Approach your own emotions with the same patience and understanding you offer your children. Create space for your own needs and set boundaries that protect your time and energy, just as you would encourage independence in your child.

Most important of all, recognize that self-care isn't selfish—it's necessary for the well-being of your family. By nurturing your own physical and emotional health, you build the foundation to be the patient, present, and compassionate parent you want to be.

Reflective Questions

Parenting is incredibly rewarding, but it can also be demanding. In this chapter we focused on the critical importance of self-care for gentle parents. Taking care of your own physical and emotional needs ensures that you can be present, patient, and responsive to your child. The questions below invite you to explore your current self-care practices, recognize signs of burnout early, and reflect on how to prioritize your well-being. They also encourage you to think about how you can maintain a strong partnership with your partner while navigating the challenges of parenting young children.

1. Reflect on the balance between caring for your child and caring for yourself. How often do you feel that one is neglected in favor of the other?

2. How can you reframe the idea of self-care from being an indulgence to being an essential part of your parenting journey?

3. How can you create small, manageable moments for self-care even on your busiest parenting days?

4. What role does physical health (exercise, nutrition, sleep) play in your emotional well-being as a parent, and how can you prioritize these areas?

5. When you begin to feel overwhelmed, what physical or emotional signs tell you that burnout may be creeping in?

6. How can you set realistic expectations for yourself to avoid the cycle of burnout, and how can you communicate those expectations with others?

7. Reflect on how parenting has impacted your relationship with your partner. What has strengthened your bond, and where do you face challenges?

8. How do you ensure that you and your partner maintain open, honest communication about parenting stress and self-care needs?

9. What small rituals or practices can you and your partner create to stay connected, even on the busiest days?

10. How can you set aside time for each other as a couple, without feeling guilty for taking time away from parenting responsibilities?

Final Thoughts

Look Forward to Raising an Independent, Creative, and Resilient Child

As you reflect on this journey through the first critical years of your child's life, remember that gentle parenting and Montessori principles share a common goal: to nurture independence, creativity, and resilience in your child.

By understanding their development, creating environments for exploration, and leading with empathy and respect, you are giving your child the tools they need to grow into confident individuals. Whether it's setting up a prepared space for your infant to explore safely, encouraging your toddler's autonomy, or fostering emotional regulation during challenging moments, each choice you make lays a foundation for their future.

Embrace Imperfection - Gentle Parenting is a Journey, Not a Destination

Throughout this guide, I hope I've made it clear that parenting is not about perfection—it's about connection. There will be setbacks, doubts, and days when you feel stretched too thin. Your child will test limits, and, yes, you will question your own choices. That's okay.

Gentle parenting is not a checklist to complete or a target to hit; it's a mindset that invites you to respond to your child with patience, love, and understanding while showing yourself, and those around you, the same grace.

In addition to describing the principles of gentle parenting and the Montessori methods, I've shared strategies that I hope will help you navigate challenges, build strong relationships, and align with others to create a support system that works for your family.

Most importantly, you've seen how your approach to parenting can inspire confidence, curiosity, and cooperation in your child. By choosing gentleness and empathy, you are planting seeds for a lifetime of trust, connection, and growth—both in your child and in yourself.

So take a deep breath. Celebrate the small victories. Embrace the imperfect moments. And trust that you are enough.

Your intentional, compassionate parenting will make all the difference, one day at a time.

All that remains for now is for me to thank you for allowing me to share this journey with you. Never doubt for a moment that your commitment to raising confident, resilient, and creative children is one of the greatest gifts you can give—to your child, to yourself, and to the world.

Bringing it All Together - Final Reflective Questions for Your Parenting Journey

Congratulations on completing this journey through gentle parenting and Montessori principles. As you reflect on what you've learned, it's important to take a step back and think about the bigger picture. These final questions will help you integrate the key ideas from the book and inspire you to continue nurturing your child's development while also fostering your own growth. Use them to guide your next steps, and remember, the rewards of this approach will unfold over time, bringing deeper connection, joy, and fulfillment to your family.

1. Reflect on the unique strengths you bring to your parenting. How can you continue to nurture those strengths as you grow alongside your child?

2. What moments in your parenting journey have made you feel most connected to your child, and how can you create more of those moments?

3. How does the blend of gentle parenting and Montessori principles resonate with your values, and how can you use this approach to create a harmonious environment for both you and your child?

4. As your child continues to grow and change, what new opportunities for learning and connection are you most excited to explore together?

5. Looking at the long-term, how do you envision your relationship with your child evolving as you continue to apply these principles in your parenting?

6. In what ways do you hope that your parenting approach will positively influence your child's character, resilience, and ability to navigate life's challenges?

7. What kind of impact do you hope your parenting approach will have on your child's sense of self, independence, and ability to navigate the world?

8. Reflecting on your journey so far, what are the biggest rewards you've experienced from embracing a gentle, Montessori-inspired approach to parenting?

9. How can you continue to integrate the values of respect, empathy, and independence into your daily life, and what positive changes do you hope to see as a result?

10. What lasting changes do you envision that gentle parenting (with that twist of a Montessori approach) will create in your family dynamic and in your own life by prioritizing the needs of your child and maintaining your own well-being?

Sources & Further Reading

Chapter 1

- Coyne, S. M., Stockdale, L., & Nelson, D. A. (2018). The association between parenting styles and adolescent self-esteem: A longitudinal study. *Journal of Adolescence, 68*, 58-66. https://doi.org/10.1016/j.adolescence.2018.07.005

- Gottman, J. M., Katz, L. F., & Hooven, C. (1997). *Meta-emotion: How families communicate emotionally*. Mahwah, NJ: Lawrence Erlbaum Associates.

- Markham, L. (2012). *Peaceful parenting: How to raise kids without yelling, shaming, or losing your mind*. New York, NY: Penguin Group.

- Siegel, D. J., & Bryson, T. P. (2016). *The whole-brain child: 12 revolutionary strategies to nurture your child's developing mind*. New York, NY: Delacorte Press.

- Thompson, R. A. (2014). The development of the self in the family context: Perspectives on child development. In R. M. Lerner (Ed.), *Handbook of child psychology* (7th ed., Vol. 1, pp. 50-101). Hoboken, NJ: Wiley.

- de Vries, T. T. F. T. H. A. M. M. (2015). Montessori education and standardized test outcomes: A comparative analysis. *International Journal of Montessori Education, 3*(1), 1-9.

- Lillard, A. S. (2017). *Montessori: The science behind the genius*. New York, NY: Oxford University Press.

- McNerney, K. (2015). The importance of collaborative learning: A review of research. *Educational Psychology Review, 27*(2), 181-204. https://doi.org/10.1007/s10648-015-9325-8

- Montessori, M. (1949). *The Absorbent Mind*. New York, NY: Ballantine Books.

- Montessori, M. (1967). *The Discovery of the Child*. New York, NY: Ballantine Books.

- Lillard, A. S. (2017). *Montessori: The science behind the genius*. New York, NY: Oxford University Press.

- Gordon, T. (2000). *Parent Effectiveness Training: The proven program for raising responsible children*. New York, NY: HarperCollins.

- Raver, C. C., & Zigler, E. (1997). *Social competence: An untapped dimension of the Head Start legacy. American Psychologist*, 52(3), 301-309. https://doi.org/10.1037/0003-066X.52.3.301

- Schore, A. N. (2001). *The effects of a secure attachment relationship on the development of the right brain: Implications for clinical practice. Infant Mental Health Journal*, 22(1-2), 7-66. https://doi.org/10.1002/1097-0355(200101/04)22:1<7::AID-IMHJ3>3.0.CO;2-I

Chapter 2

- Ainsworth, M. D. S. (1978). *Patterns of attachment: A psychological study of the strange situation*. Hillsdale, NJ: Erlbaum.

- American Academy of Pediatrics. (2018). *Caring for Your Baby and Young Child: Birth to Age 5* (7th ed.). Bantam.

- Bowlby, J. (1969). *Attachment and Loss: Vol. 1. Attachment*. New York: Basic Books.

- Piaget, J. (1954). *The construction of reality in the child*. New York: Basic Books.

- Brazelton, T. B. (1992). *Touchpoints: Your Child's Emotional and Behavioral Development*. Reading, MA: Addison-Wesley.

- Erikson, E. H. (1950). *Childhood and Society*. New York: Norton.

- Field, T. (2014). Touch. *Developmental Review, 34*(3), 224-228.

- Karp, H. (2002). The Happiest Baby on the Block.

- Montessori, M. (1967). *The Absorbent Mind*. Holt, Rinehart, and Winston.

- Lillard, P. P. (1996). *Montessori Today: A Comprehensive Approach to Education from Birth to Adulthood*. Schocken Books.

- Narvaez, D., Panksepp, J., Schore, A. N., & Gleason, T. (Eds.). (2013). *Evolution, Early Experience and Human Development: From Research to Practice and Policy*. Oxford University Press.

- Mindell, J. A., Telofski, L. S., Wiegand, B., & Kurtz, E. S. (2015). A nightly bedtime routine: Impact on sleep in young children and maternal mood. *Sleep*, 28(12), 1561-1567.

- Montessori, M. (1967). *The Absorbent Mind*. Holt, Rinehart, and Winston.

- Lillard, P. P. (1996). *Montessori Today: A Comprehensive Approach to Education from Birth to Adulthood*. Schocken Books.

- Narvaez, D., Panksepp, J., Schore, A. N., & Gleason, T. (Eds.). (2013). *Evolution, Early Experience and Human Development: From Research to Practice and Policy*. Oxford University Press.

- White, B.L., et al. (1995). "Vestibular Stimulation and Sleep in Infants," Developmental Psychobiology.

Chapter 3

- Chall, J. S. (2000). *The academic achievement challenge: What really works in the classroom*. The Guilford Press.

- Froebel, F. (2004). *The pedagogy of the kindergarten*. Cambridge University Press. (Original work published 1871)

- Gray, P. (2013). *Free to learn: Why unleashing the instinct to play will make our children happier, more self-reliant, and better students for life*. Basic Books.

- Lillard, A. S. (2017). *Montessori: The science behind the genius* (3rd ed.). Oxford University Press.

- Lillard, A. S., & Else-Quest, N. (2006). The early years: Evaluating Montessori education. *Science, 313*(5795), 1893–1894. https://doi.org/10.1126/science.1132362

- Miller, E., & Almon, J. (2009). *Crisis in the kindergarten: Why children need to play in school*. The Alliance for Childhood.

- Pica, R. (2011). *Moving and learning across the curriculum: More than 300 activities and games to make learning fun*. Pearson.

- Perry, B. D., & Szalavitz, M. (2006). *The boy who was raised as a dog: And other stories from a child psychiatrist's notebook*. Basic Books.

- Shonkoff, J. P., & Phillips, D. A. (2000). *From neurons to neighborhoods: The science of early childhood development*. National Academy Press.

- Trevarthen, C. (2001). *The neurobiology of early communication: Empathy and joint attention*. In P. J. Mundy & C. D. Masters (Eds.), *Joint attention and social cognition* (pp. 41–54). MIT Press.

- Vygotsky, L. S. (1978). *Mind in society: The development of higher psychological processes*. Harvard University Press.

- Wertsch, J. V. (1998). *Mind as action*. Oxford University Press.

Chapter 4

- Dosman, C. F., Gallagher, S., Andrews, D., & Goulden, K. J. (2020). Parenting principles primer. *Paediatrics & Child Health*, 24(2), e78–e87. https://doi.org/10.1093/pch/pxz026

- Montessori School of Downtown. (2023, December 19). Social and emotional development in toddlers. https://www.montessoridowntown.com/development-in-toddlers/

- Autonomous Kids. (n.d.). Unlock success with positive parenting tips for toddlers. https://autonomouskids.com/positive-parenting-tips-for-toddlers/

- Project Montessori. (n.d.). Montessori social and emotional learning (SEL): Nurturing empathy, conflict resolution, and self-awareness in children. https://www.projectmontessori.com/es/pages/montessori-social-and-emotional-learning-sel-nurturing-empathy-conflict-resolution-and-self-awareness-in-children

- Julianna Yuri. (n.d.). Developing social skills in toddlers: A guide for parents. https://juliannayuri.com/developing-social-skills-in-toddlers-a-guide-for-parents/

- Lee, E. J., & Kim, D. H. (2023). Effects of emotion coaching group programme for mothers of preschool children with smart device overdependence: A mixed methods study. *BMC Nursing*, 22, Article 15. https://doi.org/10.1186/s12912-023-01554-9

- Parents. (2024, October 5). 15 low-key shows for toddlers that won't overstimulate them. https://www.parents.com/low-stimulation-shows-for-toddlers-8732719

- The Atlantic. (2024, September 15). To play or not to play with your kid? https://www.theatlantic.com/family/archive/2024/09/independent-play-advice-is-stressing-parents-out/679706/

Chapter 5

- Blandon, A. Y., & Volling, B. L. (2008). Parental gentle guidance and children's compliance within the family: A replication study. *Journal of Family Psychology*, 22(3), 355–366. https://doi.org/10.1037/0893-3200.22.3.355

- Kennedy, B. (2022). *Good Inside: A Guide to Becoming the Parent You Want to Be*. Harper Wave.

- Lansbury, J. (2014). *No Bad Kids: Toddler Discipline Without Shame*. JLML Press.

- Lillard, A. S. (2017). Montessori: The science behind the genius. *Oxford University Press*.

- Ockwell-Smith, S. (2016). *The Gentle Parenting Book: How to Raise Calmer, Happier Children from Birth to Seven*. Piatkus.

- Ockwell-Smith, S. (2017). *The Gentle Discipline Book: How to Raise Co-operative, Polite and Helpful Children*. Piatkus.

- Skenazy, L. (2009). *Free-Range Kids: Giving Our Children the Freedom We Had Without Going Nuts with Worry*. Jossey-Bass.

- Sobe, N. W. (2021). The global reception of Montessori education: An analysis of the role of the Association Montessori Internationale. *Globalisation, Societies and Education*, 19(1), 1-14. https://doi.org/10.108 0/14767724.2020.1711767

Chapter 6

- Bronson, P., & Merryman, A. (2009). *NurtureShock: New thinking about children*. Twelve.

- Grusec, J. E., & Hastings, P. D. (Eds.). (2015). *Handbook of socialization: Theory and research* (2nd ed.). Guilford Publications.

- Lansford, J. E. (2017). Intergenerational support and parenting practices. *Journal of Family Studies, 23*(2), 195–207. https://doi.org/10.1080/13229 400.2017.1286668

- Macdonald, M. (2017). Aligning parenting styles with Montessori: A practical approach. *Montessori Life, 29*(1), 8–12.

- Montessori, M. (1912). *The Montessori method*. Frederick A. Stokes Company.

- Siegel, D. J., & Bryson, T. P. (2020). *The power of showing up: How parental presence shapes who our kids become and how their brains get wired*. Ballantine Books.

Chapter 7

- Adler, A., & Fagley, N. S. (2005). Appreciating gratitude: A review of the role of gratitude in psychological and physical well-being. *Journal of Personality, 73*(1), 67–97. https://doi.org/10.1111/j.1467-6494.2004.00305.x

- Basso, J. C., & Suzuki, W. A. (2017). The effects of acute exercise on mood, cognition, neurophysiology, and neurochemical pathways: A review. *Brain Plasticity, 2*(2), 127–152. https://doi.org/10.3233/BPL-160040

- Bianchi, S. M., & Milkie, M. A. (2010). Work and family research in the first decade of the 21st century. *Journal of Marriage and Family, 72*(3), 705–725. https://doi.org/10.1111/j.1741-3737.2010.00726.x

- Center for the Developing Child at Harvard University. (2016). Building the skills adults need for life: A guide for practitioners. Retrieved from https://developingchild.harvard.edu/resources/building-the-skills-adults-need-for-life/

- Ceka, A., & Murati, R. (2016). The role of parents in the education of children. *Journal of Education and Practice, 7*(5), 61–64. https://eric.ed.gov/?id=EJ1092391

- Crnic, K., & Low, C. (2002). Everyday stresses and parenting. In M. H. Bornstein (Ed.), *Handbook of parenting: Practical issues in parenting* (pp. 243–267). Mahwah, NJ: Lawrence Erlbaum Associates.

- Emmons, R. A., & Mishra, A. (2011). Why gratitude enhances well-being: What we know, what we need to know. In K. M. Sheldon, T. B. Kashdan, & M. F. Steger (Eds.), *Designing positive psychology: Taking stock and moving forward* (pp. 248–262). Oxford University Press.

- Goldstein, R. R., & Adams, L. T. (2016). The importance of social support in reducing parental stress. *Parenting: Science and Practice, 16*(1), 22–39. https://doi.org/10.1080/15295192.2016.1128305

- Holt-Lunstad, J., Smith, T. B., & Layton, J. B. (2010). Social relationships and mortality risk: A meta-analytic review. *PLoS Medicine, 7*(7), e1000316. https://doi.org/10.1371/journal.pmed.1000316

- Iwasaki, Y., Messina, E. S., & Hopper, T. (2018). Leisure, resilience, and wellness: A strengths-based perspective on mental health recovery. *Annals of Leisure Research, 21*(2), 216–227. https://doi.org/10.1080/11745398.2018.1430595

- Kabat-Zinn, J. (1990). *Full catastrophe living: Using the wisdom of your body and mind to face stress, pain, and illness*. New York, NY: Dell Publishing.

- Montessori, M. (1967). *The discovery of the child*. New York, NY: Ballantine Books.

- Neff, K. D. (2011). Self-compassion, self-esteem, and well-being. *Social and Personality Psychology Compass, 5*(1), 1–12. https://doi.org/10.1111/j.1751-9004.2010.00330.x

- Penedo, F. J., & Dahn, J. R. (2005). Exercise and well-being: A review of mental and physical health benefits associated with physical activity. *Current Opinion in Psychiatry, 18*(2), 189–193. https://doi.org/10.1097/00001504-200503000-00013

- Perry, B. D., & Szalavitz, M. (2017). *The boy who was raised as a dog: And other stories from a child psychiatrist's notebook*. New York, NY: Basic Books.

- Rao, A., & Singh, K. (2021). Yoga nidra as a stress management intervention: A scoping review. *Journal of Mental Health and Human Behavior, 26*(2), 95–102. https://doi.org/10.4103/jmhhb.jmhhb_91_21

- Siegel, D. J., & Bryson, T. P. (2012). *The whole-brain child: 12 revolutionary strategies to nurture your child's developing mind*. New York, NY: Bantam.

- World Health Organization. (2020). Parenting in the time of COVID-19. Retrieved from https://www.who.int/news-room/campaigns/connecting-the-world-to-combat-coronavirus/healthyathome/healthyathome---parenting